Franco Maria Ricci
A Labyrinth of Beauty

Num. i

А Б В Г Д
Е Ж З И І
К Л М Н
О П Р С Т
У Ф Х Ц Ч
Ш Щ Ъ Ы
Ѣ Э Ю Я

Franco Maria Ricci
A Labyrinth of Beauty

by
Antony Shugaar

VENDOME

NEW YORK · LONDON

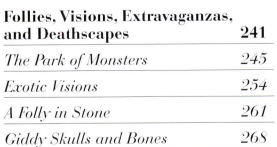

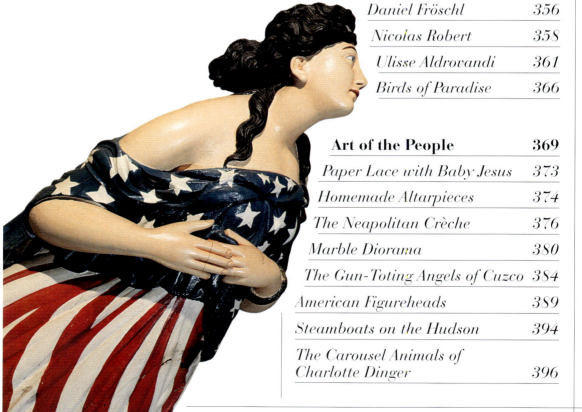

FMR✤

Internazionale   English edition

No. 1

Watteau
Zoll Zoo
Farnese Illusion
The Carrousel of the King
The Bath of Diana

Foreword
by Laura Casalis Ricci

The film director Federico Fellini came up with a lovely sobriquet for our magazine, FMR. He called it "the Black Pearl." When we first laid the foundations of the magazine in 1981, our intention was to create something as refined and precious as a pearl; and undoubtedly black is the dominant note in its chromatic scale, the background against which every artwork glitters like a full moon. There is one other characteristic that FMR shares with a pearl, namely, the nature of its birth. For a pearl is engendered by some factor of irritation, a tiny grain of sand that manages to insinuate itself between the two hinged halves of an oyster. The same was true of our magazine. Franco Maria Ricci and I regularly created wondrous books of art, and countless were the bodies of work that passed through our hands. We lavished immense care and rigor on each of them, because we wanted all our books to be—as the sadly imperfect turn of phrase would have it—perfect. Only a select few of those subjects and bodies of work finally took the form of a finished book; all too many lay incomplete, but never forgotten, and in time these relics became factors of irritation, grains of sand whose presence became too nettlesome to ignore. Because we loved each of those artistic creations or oeuvres, *they continued to appear before our eyes with all their insolent beauty, replete with the fabulous tales of those who had created that beauty and also of those who had, in their turn, discovered it. Secreted around those artists and explorers, in the oceanic depths of our publishing house, the Pearl was born.*

Thus, FMR springs from a cornucopia of excess, from the surfeit of gorgeous things that washed up on our shore, before our wondering eyes, and that over the spinning calendars of the years we decided to string, like so many pearls on a necklace, every thirty (or in time sixty, and eventually ninety) days, collecting them into an assortment that we published in the form of a magazine. It was a somewhat madcap exploit, a folly: creating issues of a magazine that was anything but ephemeral, in spite of its name, and as magazines are normally thought to be—subjects of fleeting interest. No, our magazine was better suited to being treasured in a library, like a book. As is sometimes the case with mad enterprises, it proved to be a hit; Franco had had such abiding confidence in our folly that he had given it his monogram, as if a beribboned wax seal: FMR (which ironically, in Ricci's second language, French, is pronounced éphémère—*ephemeral).*

As I write this, the man who was born with those initials is no longer among us. What has outlived him is the magazine that bears his name. We are carrying it on to the best of our abilities with the same love of beauty that almost inevitably continues to assume its natural form: that of a black pearl.

My guiding concept has always been beauty in all things, whether we're talking about a logo, an art magazine, or a book. What I wanted to create was an esthetic identity, discernment, elegance. To my mind, there is nothing without visual beauty.

Franco Maria Ricci

The World According to Franco Maria Ricci

One day in 1982, Franco Maria Ricci came to my office on East 34th Street. I was the senior editor of *Attenzione*, the Italian lifestyle monthly, and I had reached out to a contact at Rizzoli to know more about this new, ultra-spectacular art magazine, FMR. I wanted to interview Ricci for the next issue, and suddenly there he was, vintage red Bakelite rose adorning his jacket lapel, swathed in fine tailoring and a fierce glow of imagination. The interview turned on me before I knew it, and Ricci had offered me a job in Milan as he gathered up his belongings and left. It was amazing.

Everything moved quickly after that. I remember my visit to the oversized office of Rizzoli International's chief accountant, who counted out a stack of fresh hundred-dollar bills and wished me well; boarding an Alitalia flight to Milan; being ushered into my new apartment practically over the new FMR shop on Milan's central Via Durini; and visiting Franco's orange-and-gold fauxed home in Via Giason del Maino (where I met Franco's partner, the petite and terrifyingly commanding Laura Casalis), a house bedecked with black-enameled cabinetry, artwork by Erté, Art Nouveau chryselephantine (gold and ivory) statuettes of ballerinas, and immense rhinoceros-hide volumes dating from the eighteenth century. On the first day, Franco took me to lunch with a very young Patricia Gucci. Downstairs from my new home, I met the warehouseman who managed the vast stores of black-silk-bound books and magazines, but who was also in charge of the artistic *trompe-l'œil* stuccowork in the shop on Via Durini: faux-leather book spines. I later visited him in the warehouse, walking down lines of bookshelves and stumbling upon Franco's lustrous black Jaguar XKE (E-Type). It was like that scene from the end of *Citizen Kane*, reprised as the last scene in *Raiders of the Lost Ark*: a preposterous abundance of crates, each containing enigmatic treasures.

I had not yet seen the equally fabulous FMR shops in Rome, Paris, London, and New York. Some of them, indeed, lay in the future, yet to take form.

What was steadily being borne into me was the sheer industrial scope of what Ricci and Casalis were creating. It felt like the kind of manufactory you might find in a particularly fervid episode of the life of Baron Munchausen; not the scope of a modern multinational, but something more in keeping with an ambitious grand duke, say. Weirdly, though, it also felt as if this busy enterprise existed in two time periods at once, utterly modern if not postmodern, and exquisitely of another time, like a Baroque Brigadoon.

Ultimately, that is the magic trick that Ricci managed to pull off: presenting the past as the newest, most exciting thing around. That piece of prestidigitation was performed using several pieces of stagecraft. One was the sheer quality of production.

Ricci was proud to claim many friends of FMR, and among their number was Jacqueline Kennedy Onassis, who called FMR "the most beautiful

magazine in the world." Jackie O knew whereof she spoke when it came to books and to esthetic presentation, and she actually collaborated with Ricci on his production of a facsimile edition of Bodoni's *Oratio Dominica*, an 1806 typographic production of the Lord's Prayer in 155 languages (and their various scripts).

Another friend of FMR was film director Federico Fellini, who called the magazine "the Black Pearl," a loving reference to the special fifth ink used in printing it. FMR black is not exactly glossy or matte; it serves the same function that Byzantine gold performs, as an ethereal background. It places the subject of each page in a timeless, floating world. Fellini was a swashbuckling showman who not only recognized the Riccian touchstones of transcendence, lost causes, and unreasonable ambition, but also relied on the rumpled elegance of such actors as Marcello Mastroianni, who shared Ricci's easy *sprezzatura*. FMR was a Noah's ark of artistic beauty, but also a code of dandyish fine manners, offering lessons in nonchalant appreciation of the lovely and gracious.

So the glossy, enameled black of that fifth ink marked FMR out as a visual machine, a strange inverse camera obscura, a Cornell box from which to roll out an endlessly replenished Wunderkammer of surprises.

The late, visionary Italian essayist and novelist Alberto Arbasino nailed the oddly evocative content of the FMR time machine, what John Lennon once described (referencing the light and beauty of San Francisco) as "living in a memory." He described what he imagined as the typical delivery device of an issue of FMR: a mounted messenger, dressed head to foot in glossy black, hip boots, jumpsuit, and visored helmet, arriving in a futuristic aircar with a copy of the magazine in a courier's satchel.

But it was really Ricci's empathetic reach—the negative capability that allowed him to see the present as something that hadn't yet happened—that so powerfully guided his curatorial instincts.

There is a powerful online tool for exploring the emergence of language and thought: Google's Ngram viewer. Surveying virtually the entire corpus of printed books, it does a reasonable job of dating the advent of new phrases and expressions. One term that begins swimming into view right around 1982 is "world-building."

After the decades of "all that is solid melts into air," Ricci was looking past the fanfare of the new and pioneering a cornucopia of the unfamiliar but astonishing nuggets that the past has to offer. In those days, perhaps, denizens of the present—accustomed to the vast store of faulty knowledge about the past—simply thought of bygone worlds as sleepy, dusty places, poorly reflected in the artifacts that survived: daguerreotypes, faded portraits of what the poet Philip Larkin called "fools in old-style hats and coats." But Ricci was excavating manuscripts, monuments, statuary, and archival periodicals from the ark of old culture and giving them their star turns, their Cecil B. DeMille close-ups.

Even now, lulled by the comfort of living atop the klieg light of our immense present-day store of knowledge (not unlike those vast warehouses of dusty crates from *Citizen Kane* and *Raiders of the Lost Ark*), we still unwisely judge everything stereotypical and quaint from the past as it lies swathed and flattened in that dictatorial glare. The past has little recourse,

BORGES
A/Z

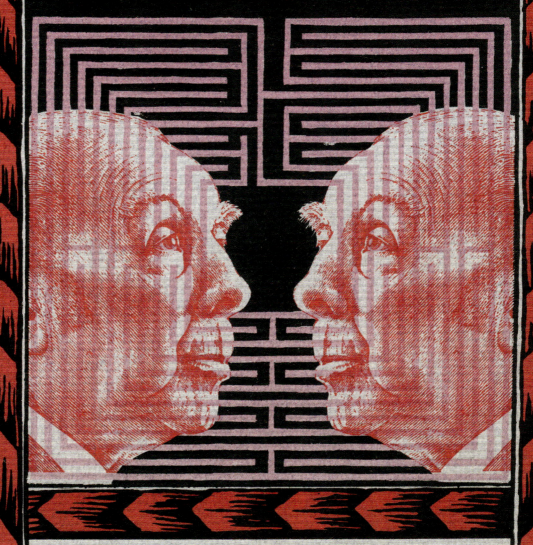

La Biblioteca di Babele
collana di letture fantastiche
diretta da Jorge Luis Borges

Franco Maria Ricci editore

no voice to defend its depth and brilliance. Ricci, with an insight rarely found among magazine publishers, methodically spoke for those magical centuries.

Those faces in old-fashioned hats and coats were actually blinking in awe, excitedly captivated by the radiant prospects of future ages. Where are *their* aircars, where the globe-spanning luxury dirigible airships? What do we have to offer that's so damned magical? I'd make a modest nomination of FMR itself, a daringly futuristic piece of printing technology and artistic sensibility.

Do we, the living, owe the past a collective letter of apology? Well, nobody wrote a finer thank-you note to past centuries and millennia than Franco Maria Ricci.

The Treasure-House of Parma

The arc of Ricci's life, from place of origin to final, sprawling expanse, both embodies and explains his remarkable ability to see art and allow others to see it with him. He landed, as if a visitor from some otherworldly plane, in a city of remarkable romantic appeal and profound artistic roots. With apologies to Stendhal (whose name has been invoked to describe the state of numbed frenzy induced by a surfeit of artistic beauty), the publisher of FMR was born into the treasure house of Parma. His hometown imbued him with a vast array of cultural touchstones. First among many, perhaps, is the remarkable work of the typographer Giambattista Bodoni, but also the very aura of Parma under the redoubtable Duchess Marie Louise, second wife of Napoleon Bonaparte; the stunning Teatro Farnese that opens this book (followed by a double page of Bodoni's fonts); the city's Romanesque architecture (especially the Baptistery, with the noteworthy thirteenth-century work of sculptor Benedetto Antelami); such great painters as Correggio, who worked at the height of the Renaissance but foreshadowed and inspired the Baroque and Rococo eras that would follow (pages 6–7); and of course Parmigianino, nicknamed by artists in Rome—whether affectionately or mockingly—for the city itself (the name means, literally, Little Parma).

None of these eras was alien to Ricci from childhood, but it was in particular the Parma of Marie Louise that touched Ricci's sensibilities. The duchess herself was written out of Stendhal's novel *The Charterhouse of Parma* (1839), replaced by a conniving duke. (Perhaps to any admirer of the first French emperor, and certainly to Stendhal, painting her as a moral defective would have been an act of lese-majesty.)

As a very young man, Ricci was encouraged by his father to pursue an artistic self-education. He was regularly given the train fare to travel to what Italians call "cities of art" for what constituted a youthful graduate seminar in the fine craft of seeing. In Ricci's own words, "I grew up surrounded by my father's books. Reading Shakespeare, Homer, Joyce, and Dante saved me from bad taste. It made beauty simple, familiar, and immediate in my eyes."

Another factor in Ricci's formation was an almost reckless love of adventure. He had initially set his heart on becoming an archaeologist, but was persuaded by an uncle to study geology instead. The realities of geology, however, with

CHESTERTON

L'occhio di Apollo

La Biblioteca di Babele

*collana di letture fantastiche
diretta da Jorge Luis Borges*

Franco Maria Ricci editore

E. A. POE
La lettera rubata

La Biblioteca di Babele
*collana di letture fantastiche
diretta da Jorge Luis Borges*

Franco Maria Ricci editore

dull months of unsuccessful prospecting in Turkey for Gulf Oil, persuaded him that another path was in order. He ventured into the high-pitched, high-speed, keening and dangerous circuits of road and track racing, but one day, as he stood chatting with Enzo Ferrari, he saw a fellow driver die in a crash. He'd been waiting for that driver to pull in so that he could take the wheel of that very race car. All things considered, other creative outlets beckoned.

A chance encounter with an American curator working on an Italian design show in New York led Ricci into the field of graphic design in 1963. Ricci's clients included Alitalia (striking and highly artistic airline tickets), department store Neiman Marcus, the Italian post office, and such design-forward appliance manufacturers as SCIC Italia and Smeg (both based in Parma). He also published a seven-volume collection of great design: *Top Symbols and Trademarks of the World* (1973). Organized by country (volume seven includes Sweden and Socialist Countries), the series features 7,000 logos and trademarks, and was itself an encyclopedic lookbook that foreshadowed his world-evoking, programmatic work as a publisher.

Facsimiles of Volumes Past

But let's not skip over the foundational works in Ricci's career as a publisher. Even as his graphic design career was blossoming, his publishing work was waxing ambitious and idiosyncratic. He started out by publishing a facsimile edition of Bodoni's classic *Manuale Tipografico* (1818), laying down a marker by emulating his esthetic hero. Ricci's twentieth-century edition was published in 1964, and required efforts mingling the latest technology of the time with manual ingenuity to reproduce the printing blocks.

(Although Ricci's friendship with the Argentinian writer Jorge Luis Borges comes later, the parallel with the short story "Pierre Menard, Author of the *Quixote*" is unmistakable and demands mention: far easier for Cervantes, a seventeenth-century Spaniard, to write *Don Quixote*, than the awesome challenge taken on by Borges' Menard: to be a twentieth-century Frenchman and yet write the exact same text. As Borges puts it: "Menard, a contemporary of William James, defines history not as a *delving into* reality but as the very *fount* of reality." Ricci's heroic effort to re-create Bodoni's magnum opus exactly as his hero fashioned it, but using twentieth-century tools, is the ultimate swashbuckling escapade in art publishing.)

Over six hundred plates, letters in Latin and "exotic" alphabets, and more than a thousand ornaments and engraved borders: Ricci described Bodoni's work as a two-dimensional equivalent of Canova's statuary. He purchased a pair of offset typesetting machines, spending more on these machines (which were advanced for their time) than he would have paid for his dream car, a Ferrari: unquestionable proof of his devotion to the project. Special bespoke Fabriano paper was developed for the project. Commercially, too, this was risky adventure of a particularly refined variety. But the nine hundred volumes sold like hotcakes.

TAROTS

The Visconti Pack in Bergamo and New York

Text by Italo Calvino

Franco Maria Ricci

TAMARA
DE LEMPICKA

*Col diario della governante
di Gabriele d'Annunzio*

Franco Maria Ricci editore

Ricci's next anastatic undertaking was a reprint of Bodoni's *Oratio Dominica*, the refined Latin title of the Lord's Prayer (not to be confused with the homelier *paternoster*, literally "our father"). The original *Oratio Dominica* was created by 1806, as we have seen, with the short prayer reproduced in 155 languages. The facsimile, which is still available for €4,000, is said to be "the most extensive catalogue of alphabets and typefaces ever printed." Ricci stepped up his international marketing with text by UN Secretary General U Thant and Pope Paul VI. Enjoying the glamorous patronage of Jacqueline Kennedy, each volume was signed by both world-renowned authors, and proceeds were donated to restoration efforts following the catastrophic flood of the Arno in Florence in 1966.

Ricci devoted the 1970s to the publication of an even more ambitious facsimile: the eighteen volumes of Diderot and d'Alembert's *Encyclopédie*, a project that won him the recognition of the French government. He was dubbed a Chevalier de la République Française in 1982, and later elevated to a commander of that order.

During those same years, Ricci began publishing illustrated books in a handsome, lucent-black, faux-silk binding with gold-embossed Bodoni lettering and tipped-in color plates. The subjects were pioneering at the time, largely overlooked; now they are popular if not canonical. Perhaps, though, it's not so much a matter of Ricci having been ahead of his time. Rather, it might have been that Ricci himself elevated these subjects and taught the world to see them. Once he'd published them, they could no longer *help* but be seen.

Among them were, in 1969, Italo Calvino's text on the Visconti deck of Tarot cards, which the author later expanded to become *The Castle of Crossed Destinies*; in 1972, a book on the Art Deco designer Erté, with text by Roland Barthes; in 1973, the codices of Beatus of Liébana, with text by Umberto Eco; in 1977, a volume of the art of Tamara de Lempicka, with notes by Gabriele D'Annunzio's housekeeper; and in 1981, the *Codex Seraphinianus* by Luigi Serafini.

In the mid-1970s, Ricci decided to follow his personal compass and flew to Buenos Aires, basically setting up camp outside of the office of the head librarian of the Biblioteca Nacional Mariano Moreno, none other than his second great hero (and, unlike Bodoni, still living): Jorge Luis Borges. Borges welcomed him warmly and guided him (blind though he was) on a sightseeing tour of the magnificent building. Working his persuasive campaign, Ricci had soon persuaded Borges to visit him in his home in the countryside near Parma, and gleefully accompanied him to Geneva, Borges' longed-for dreamland and ideal homeland. Ricci's courtship paid off, and Borges began working with Ricci's publishing house as the curator of a series titled "La Biblioteca di Babele"—The Library of Babel.

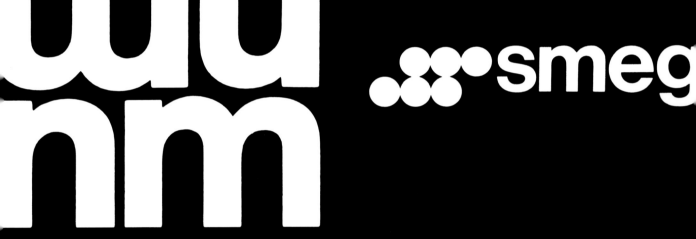

smeg

SCIC

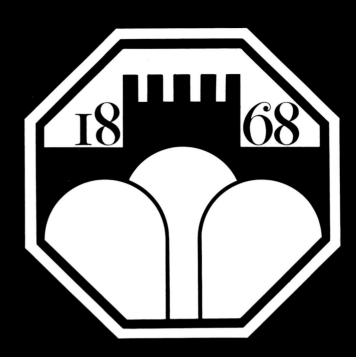

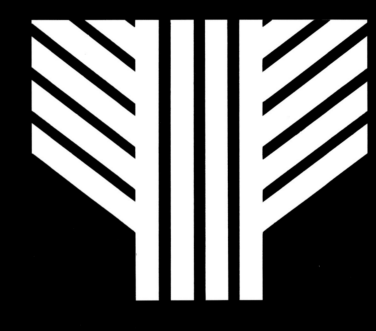

KOS

Vol. III   settembre 1986   Lit. 5000

N. 25
Tropico degli insetti
Sibylla Merian
entomopittrice nel Surinam

Franco Maria Ricci

FMR

mensile di Franco Maria Ricci   settembre 1983

N.16

Le belle tasse
Il volto di Shiva
Il silenzio e la città
Islam Pop
Liberty in banca

FMR ✿

International   English edition

No. 1

Borgesian Exploits

By this point in Ricci's personal history (as we approach the day I met him and tried to interview him, only to be interviewed and hired by him instead), he had been sharing both his work and his personal life for a number of years with Laura Casalis. If there are parallels in Ricci's life to Stendhal and to Borges, I also glimpse a hint of the story of a fictional character, one who is particularly meaningful as a trope to the Italian intellectual public: Daniel Defoe's Robinson Crusoe. Instead of being stranded on the island of Más Afuera, this marooned mariner washed up in the countryside outside of Parma, notoriously one of the richest and most livable culinary and cultural oases on Earth. Ricci as Crusoe, therefore, had the luxury of re-creating his own versions of not palm-leaf huts and stockades, but Enlightenment compendiums and highly evolved exercises of the printer's and typographer's arts. Again, a Pierre Menard or Fabrizio del Dongo reviving an ideal world and living in it his own romantic, swaggering cavalcade of adventures. There to assist this stranded DIY aesthete was his Girl Friday: Laura Casalis.

The next logical step was a magazine. Assembling the team meant reaching out to his familiar friends and collaborators: photographer Massimo Listri, writer Italo Calvino, gifted editorial hands and authors in their own right Gianni Guadalupi and Giovanni Mariotti, and a squad of other remarkable individuals, many of whom it was my privilege to get to know upon my arrival in Milan in late 1983. I worked with William Weaver, who had translated the writings of Calvino and Eco's *The Name of the Rose* (1980), and who came to work in our editorial office regularly. I learned to translate from one of the best.

Franco and Laura founded the original, Italian edition of FMR in March 1982. In the first issue, among other articles, there was a sampling of Serafini's *Codex Seraphinianus*, accompanied by Calvino's text. Serafini wooed Ricci, who loved what he saw; Calvino, invited to write about it, was equally delighted. If the facsimiles harked back to the imitation game at play in Bodoni's manual and Menard's *Don Quixote*, then Serafini signaled forward to the world-building of FMR. His Borgesian world of nonsensical but evocative images and asemic text (characterized by a "vacuum of meaning") seems to allude to a parallel universe that has forgotten about us, the reader.

There is a hierarchical order to every page of FMR. The special black ink seems to make every image resemble the actual thing as glimpsed through the viewfinder of a large-format camera. The photography, as I learned during my brief travels with Listri, are almost uniformly shot with large-format cameras, and are hieratically frontal, without angle or human presence. Even the matte varnish on the black and polychromatic pages offers an entrancing detail, making it appear as though any reflection of the outside world glimpsed on a page of FMR is viewed through the slightly frosted glass of an old-fashioned Rolleiflex.

PARMA
15° FESTIVAL
INTERNAZIONALE
DEL TEATRO
UNIVERSITARIO
11/19 MARZO
1967

Alitalia
Issued by Alitalia, Roma, IATA *member*

Biglietto passeggeri e ricevuta bagaglio
Passenger ticket and baggage check

Alitalia
Issued by Alitalia, Roma, IATA *member*

Biglietto passeggeri e ricevuta bagaglio
Passenger ticket and baggage check

Alitalia
Issued by Alitalia, Roma, IATA *member*

Biglietto passeggeri e ricevuta bagaglio
Passenger ticket and baggage check

Alitalia
Issued by Alitalia, Roma, IATA *member*

Biglietto passeggeri e ricevuta bagaglio
Passenger ticket and baggage check

Alitalia
Issued by Alitalia, Roma, IATA *member*

Biglietto passeggeri e ricevuta bagaglio
Passenger ticket and baggage check

Alitalia
Issued by Alitalia, Roma, IATA *member*

Biglietto passeggeri e ricevuta bagaglio
Passenger ticket and baggage check

Alitalia
Issued by Alitalia, Roma, IATA *member*

Biglietto passeggeri e ricevuta bagaglio
Passenger ticket and baggage check

Alitalia
Issued by Alitalia, Roma, IATA *member*

Biglietto passeggeri e ricevuta bagaglio
Passenger ticket and baggage check

Alitalia
Issued by Alitalia, Roma, IATA *member*

Biglietto passeggeri e ricevuta bagaglio
Passenger ticket and baggage check

Alitalia
Issued by Alitalia, Roma, IATA *member*

Biglietto passeggeri e ricevuta bagaglio
Passenger ticket and baggage check

Alitalia
Issued by Alitalia, Roma, IATA *member*

Biglietto passeggeri e ricevuta bagaglio
Passenger ticket and baggage check

Alitalia
Issued by Alitalia, Roma, IATA *member*

Biglietto passeggeri e ricevuta bagaglio
Passenger ticket and baggage check

Phantasmagorical Stage Set

I had seen copies of the magazine before coming to Milan, but it was quite another matter to see it in its context. The offices were in Palazzo Visconti di Modrone, where the filmmaker Luchino Visconti had grown up. Stunningly elegant and courtly though the rooms were, even more impressive was the furniture, designed by Ricci himself, with a matte-black glow instilled in the enameled paint, as if on the pages of the magazine itself. One particularly impressive piece of furniture that Ricci had designed was a ceiling-height flat file structure that contained large, shallow, black plastic trays perfect for holding galleys and printing proofs.

The whole phantasmagorical machinery behind FMR seemed like an elaborate stage set, designed to conjure up a world. And that world, when conjured, took the form of FMR magazine. The covers were stunning, laid out against a black enamel field that conveyed timelessness and infinity with the same majesty that Byzantine art had drawn from its gold backgrounds. One after another, they strode boldly out into the world: a chased golden head gazing placidly from what turns out to have been an *aquamanile*, a medieval water dispenser; a Persian acrobat turning a handspring in a piece of Qajar art; another golden figure, this one an Art Deco faun from Gabriele D'Annunzio's incredible lakeside home; a vintage slot machine adorned with bright red and yellow Art Nouveau cloisonné darts; a vivid scientific illustration of a flying fish by the sixteenth-century naturalist Ulisse Aldrovandi; a fierce-faced be-turbaned Moorish figure with two tame baboons on leashes, a character from a spectacular eighteenth-century Neapolitan crèche. On and on it went, ending only in 2007, when Ricci grew restless and decided to build the world's largest bamboo labyrinth on his property outside of Parma (along with a world-class museum to house his collection, and an observation tower and pyramid—no doubt Borges would have been proud). Those 163 issues amount to an encyclopedia of the marvelous, the bizarre, and the serendipitous: more than 20,000 pages, which, combined with the 127 issues of the English-language edition (16,000 pages or more) and the shorter runs of the French and the Spanish editions, produce something equivalent in page count to the legendary eleventh edition of the *Encyclopaedia Britannica*.

Franco and Laura could safely rest on their laurels at this point. FMR had always been a compendium of the jewels and miracles of the past, often new discoveries or revivals of the overlooked, but it was something more. Each issue—improvised and assembled in a breathless, stunning act of last-minute legerdemain (I will never forget seeing the two of them one evening, newly arrived from the airport after a grueling flight from Java, completely revamping the bluelines of the latest issue, which was going to press the next day)—was, rather than a compilation of ancient and vintage art, actually a work of late twentieth-century performance art.

But the greatest exploit was the launch of the magazine in what Ricci had dubbed Operation Columbus. We'll cover that at the end of this book. It was a truly spectacular piece of marketing, worthy of the greatest entertainments, jousts, and carousels of the crowned heads of Europe.

The Masone Labyrinth

It is fitting for the structure of Ricci's life, for the continued existence and success of the magazine, and perhaps in a sense for this essay, to close with a delightfully ambiguous denouement, the story of the Masone Labyrinth and Museum.

Ricci was a classicist, or a neoclassicist, but in a very real way his interests were strangely chthonic, not imbued with the linear, positivist sunlight of the Enlightenment. Much has been made of the difference between the stained-glass windows of the Middle Ages and the sun-drenched galleries of Versailles, which boasts 2,513 windows and 483 mirrors, most of those face-to-face with arched windows. (Someone once noted that Venice has a special relationship with sunlight because of the canals, which reflect it, effectively doubling the city's harvest of luminosity. Versailles seems to have been attempting to double-dip in much the same fashion.)

Ricci might have looked at this effort and traced not the light, but the glass on a transverse path. He would have appreciated the manifold permutations of glass itself, as a filter both for light and for darkness. He might have appreciated Emily Dickinson's advice to "tell all the truth but tell it slant." He might have remembered the note Gertrude Stein wrote on her final exam for a class taught by William James, brother of the writer Henry James: "Dear Professor James, I am so sorry but really I do not feel a bit like an examination paper in philosophy today." Despite this, Stein received the highest mark in the course, along with a note from Professor James: "Dear Miss Stein, I understand perfectly how you feel. I often feel like that myself."

Ricci's departure from the editorship of FMR was less light-hearted, but it too partook of the same quixotic, other-oriented spirit. Laura and Franco had sold the magazine to a close friend, on the understanding that they would continue to run it editorially. Sadly, finance had a vote, and to their (and their friend's) chagrin, FMR wound up in other hands. Around 2007, the magazine ceased publication.

What continued, however, was work on another project: the largest labyrinth on Earth, at least the largest consisting entirely of bamboo plants. Lest you think of a corn maze by a highway somewhere, it is much more than that. It is an elegant labyrinth, complete with refreshments, shops, suites for the night, a world-class museum certified for intermuseological loans, as well as a watchtower and a pyramid—in short, a caravanserai, albeit one alongside the Via Emilia rather than on the actual Silk Road.

Ricci being Ricci, it attracts a considerable number of visitors, roughly 100,000 a year. And, Ricci being Ricci, it embodies in a popular vehicle some of the oddest and most intriguing points of the FMR spidey-tingle: puzzlement and elation, paradox and blinding insight, bafflement (this is a genuinely diabolical maze) and liberation. Just as Serafini's asemic writing was strangely informative (the writing itself conveyed thoughts unspoken, just as lies can be unmasked by watching the liar on television with the sound off), so the perplexity of the maze can set you free in an amble through greenery and sunshine.

The adjoining museum is itself a labyrinthine tour of ideas and notions. One of my favorite exhibits, enigmatic and strangely haunting, in this Believe-It-or-Not trip through erudition and the uncanny is the fourteenth-century narwhal's horn, touted of course as that of a unicorn.

The last attraction is a pyramid, hollow and slated to hold Ricci's ashes, like the monument designed by Étienne-Louis Boullée in the midst of the Enlightenment. It summons up the opening scenes of Luc Besson's *The Fifth Element*. It is, quite literally, a strange attractor.

And you exit, appropriately, through the gift shop.

Ligabue was born in Switzerland and
led an erratic childhood and adolescence
marked by economic, physical, and mental
hardship that resulted in frequent stays in
psychiatric hospitals. He created this work
during the most prolific period of his career,
which was characterized by a bright,
audacious palette, an Expressionist use of
color, and the pronounced dark outlines
of foregrounded figures.

Happily marooned as Ricci was on the shores of his rather sumptuous desert isle, he and his Girl Friday soon found their way to the realms of beauty, scattered freely and largely overlooked by the benighted inhabitants. It was Italy in the early 1980s, and language was understood to be a *system* in a semiological world where "reality" was regularly used in the plural: *realities*. A language that takes the form of codified units of meaning, such as the various Tarot figures. Or the language expressed in the elegant letterforms devised by Giambattista Bodoni; after all, to see words printed in an elegant typeface is the visual equivalent of the orotund enunciation of a master speechmaker.

And so what better array of paintings to open with than various renditions of the Tower of Babel? Thus, a commentary on the profusion of visual vernaculars, media, cultures, and storylines, a reminder that the gods of iconography are only too happy to scramble the words on the page.

With his co-founder Italo Calvino, Ricci was fascinated by the lexicon of Tarot decks. There is a charming video on YouTube of a 1974 interview with Ricci and Calvino on RSI (Swiss radio and television), in which Ricci announces that fantastic literature might be, say, a story by Jorge Luis Borges that features an impressive writer who doesn't exist.

But the apex of visual eloquence, and the tail that the serpent bites in the ouroboros, comes with Luigi Serafini's depiction of an imaginary universe, narrated in an asemic script. As the estimable critic Justin Taylor puts it in the conclusion to his 2007 essay on Serafini's *Codex Seraphinianus* in *McSweeney's*, quoting Borges: "The metaphysicians of Tlön are not looking for truth, nor even for an approximation of it; they are after a kind of amazement. They consider metaphysics a branch of fantastic literature."

Towers of Babel

Facing page
Hendrick van Cleve III (ca. 1525–1590/95)
The Building of the Tower of Babel,
16th century
Oil on copper, 16¼ × 18¾ in
(41.3 × 47.5 cm)
Otterlo, Kröller-Müller Rijksmuseum
Courtesy of Kröller-Müller Rijksmuseum

Pages 70–71
Pieter Bruegel the Elder (ca. 1525–1569)
The (Great) Tower of Babel, 1563
Oil on wood panel, 44⅞ × 61 in
(114 × 155 cm)
Vienna, Kunsthistorisches Museum
Photograph by Meyer

Page 72
Unknown Flemish artist
The Tower of Babel, late 16th century
Oil on wood panel, diameter 17¼ in
(44 cm)
Madrid, Museo del Prado
Courtesy of Museo del Prado

Page 73
Unknown Flemish artist
The Tower of Babel, late 16th century
Oil on wood panel, 43¾ × 59½ in
(111 × 151 cm)
Mainz, Gemäldegalerie
Courtesy of Landesmuseum Mainz

Tarot as Lexicon

Pages 65 and 74–79
The "Charles VI" tarot cards
Northern Italy, late 15th century
17 cards (out of 78?), Italian suits
Ink drawing, painted, gilded and silvered,
then printed; multi-layered paper
with Italian-style turned edges; plain
solid-white backs, 7–7¼ × 3½–3¼ in
(18–18.5 × 9–9.5 cm)
Paris, Bibliothèque Nationale de France
Photographs by Jean-Marie Aragon

Page 74
Justice

Page 75
Page of Swords *(with the inscription*
"FANTE" [PAGE] on the garter)

Page 76, left to right and top to bottom:
Death, The Emperor, The Lover, Strength,
The Tower, The Fool

Page 77, left to right and top to bottom:
The Last Judgment, The World, The Pope,
The Sun, The Moon, Temperance

Page 78
The Hermit

Page 79 (and 65)
The Hanged Man

Bodoni—Font of Wisdom

Page 80
Title page of the magnificent Bodoni volume
Britannia, Lathmon, Villa Bromhamensis,
printed in Parma, 1792

Page 81
Matrices for printing types, Bodoni printing
works
Parma, Museo Bodoniano
Photograph by Brooks Walker

Pages 82–85
Cases of typefaces, Bodoni printing works
Parma, Museo Bodoniano
Photograph by Brooks Walker

The Codex Found at Milan

Pages 86–91
Luigi Serafini (born 1949)
Double-page spreads, plates from Codex
Seraphinianus, *1976–78 (first edition in two*
volumes by Franco Maria Ricci, 1981)
Colored pencils on paper, each plate
22¾ × 17 in (58 × 43 cm)
Fontanellato, Masone Labyrinth, Franco
Maria Ricci Collection

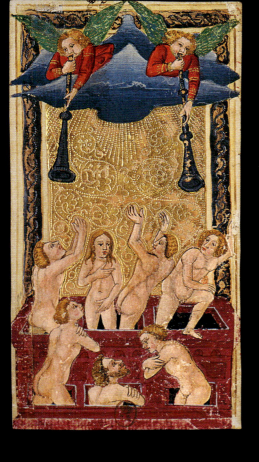

To the KING

SIR,

In obedience to the wish which Your Majesty once so graciously expressed to me, I have directed a few copies of the Britannia and two other Latin poems of my Fa-

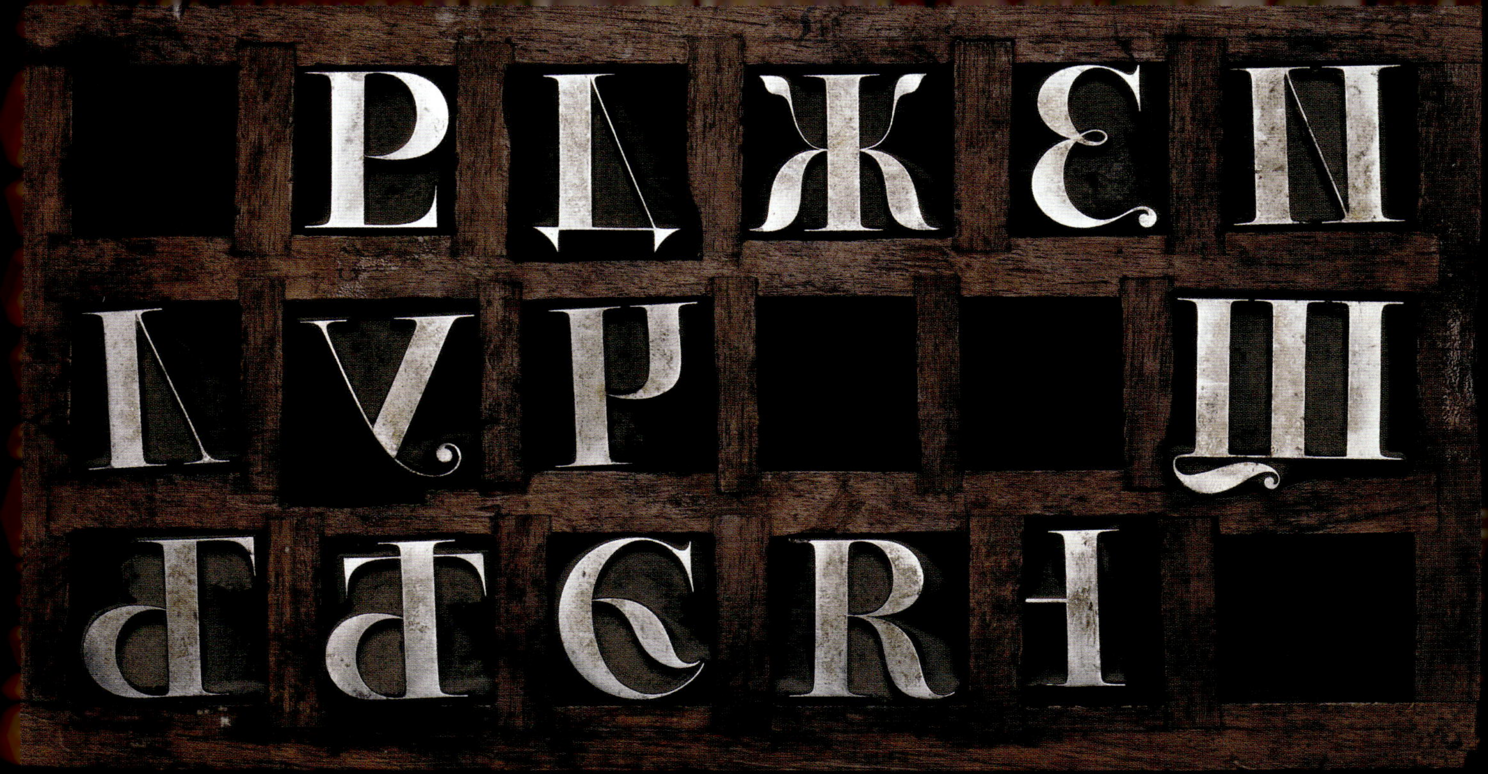

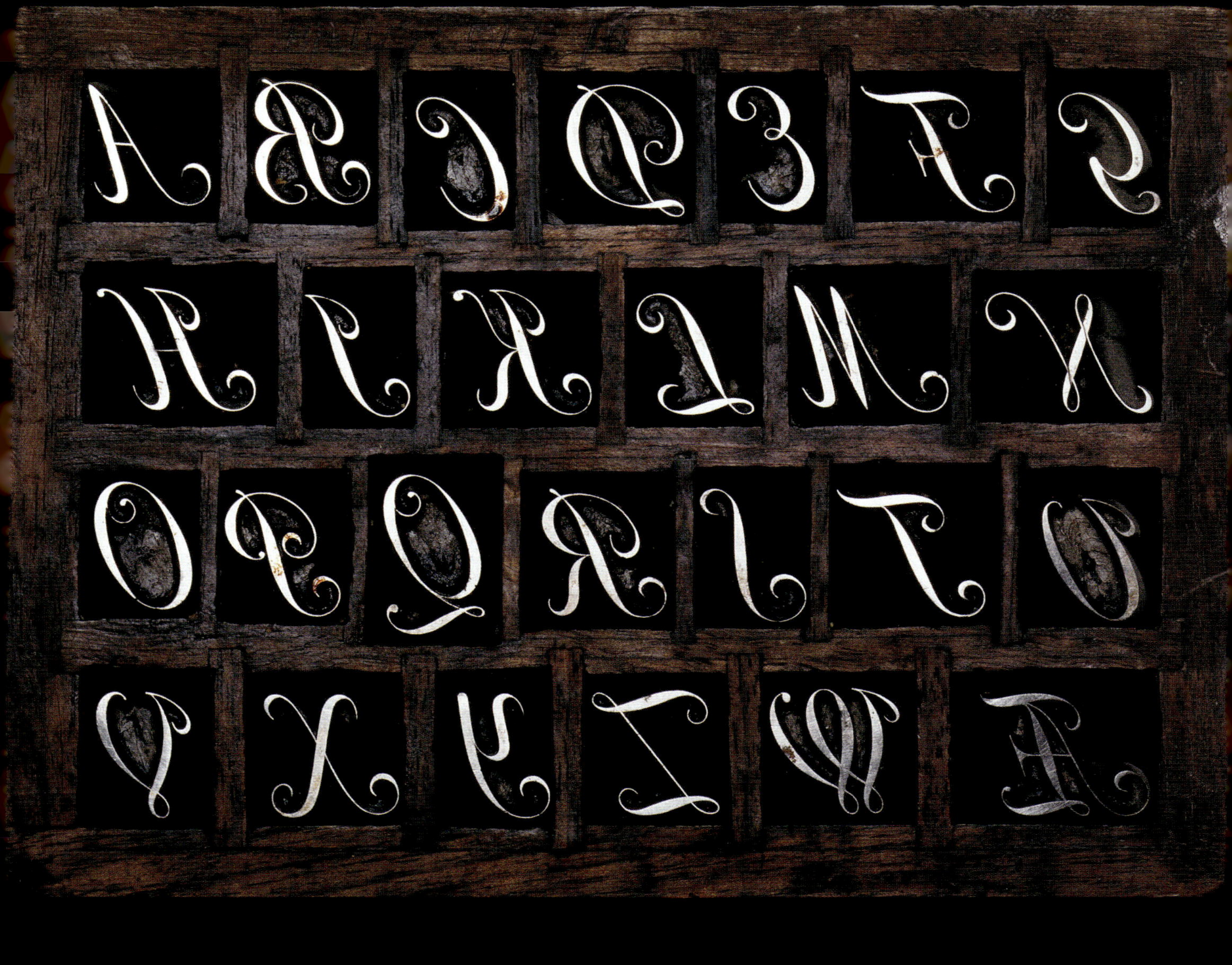

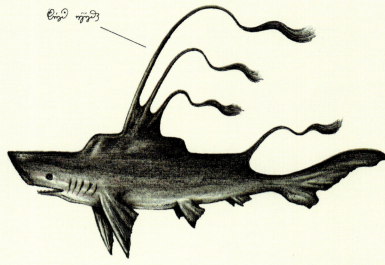

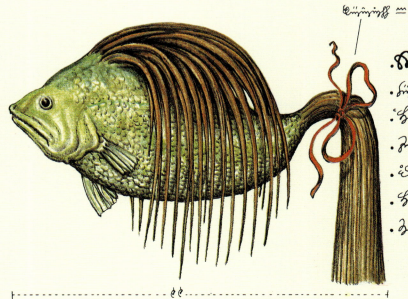

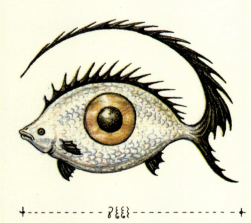

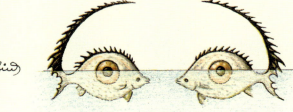

ℰi ℓɽɵℯɽℊℰⱲ ɝ ɕⱤɕℓⱱ
•ⱰⱳᵶℯɽɕℎℎⱲ ɕⱲɝ ⱤᵶℎℎℰℯⱲℓℯⱤɕⱱᵶⱱ
Ⱳ ⱲᵶℎℎℯⱤⱳℎℯᵶⱳ ⱲᵶℎℎℯⱤⱲℯⱳ ᵶ Ⱳℰ
ℂⱲⱳℎℎℰℰⱳ ℯᵶⱳⱳ ⱲⱤⱳℰⱳ ℓⱳℯⱳℎℎℰⱳⱳ ᵶ
ℎℯⱳ ᵶ ℎℰⱳ ℎℯⱳℯ ℂⱲⱳ ℯⱳⱳⱳ ℓⱳℯⱳ
ⱲⱲℎℎℯⱳⱳ ℯᵶ ℎⱳⱳⱳⱳ ᵶ Ɽⱳℎ ℥ⱳⱳⱲⱳ ℈ⱳ
ℰⱳ Ɽⱳℎℎℯⱳ Ɽⱳℎℎℯℯⱳⱳ Ɽⱳℎℯⱳⱳ ℩ℰⱳ

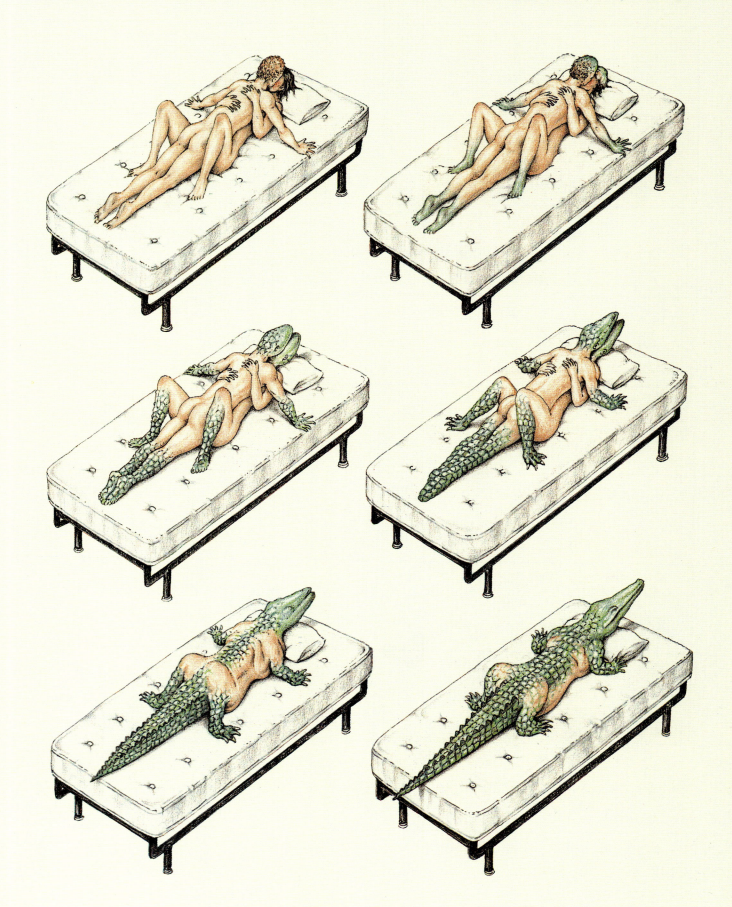

Read My Face

"**H**uman faces are an incentive to clairvoyance," writes Mark Helprin in his novel *A Winter's Tale* (1983). The many issues of FMR (163 in Italian, 127 in English) are a veritable séance of ghostly faces. This chapter offers a sampling of them in chronological order.

The mummy masks of the Egyptian oasis Fayum were placed upon the embalmed, bandage-wrapped bodies of the dead and kept in the household as repositories of beloved ancestral spirits. These painted faces are almost the only clues we have to what ancient Greek portrait painting must have looked like, a startlingly realistic and intimate glimpse of the past. Equally evocative are bronze busts of Roman emperors, a dangling satyr's mask from the Villa of Mysteries in Pompeii, and faces of the Buddha from the Gandhara region of northwestern India, a relic of the artistic skills of the Hellenic colonies left behind by Alexander the Great. Oddly, then, our earliest documentation of the face of the Buddha is distinctly Hellenistic in style.

From that syncretic depiction, we move on to the Renaissance: Giovanna Garzoni of Florence, Moretto da Brescia, and the family and household of an aging infante by the hand of Francisco Goya. Then the German Enlightenment, with the remarkable caricatural style of Franz Xaver Messerschmidt, all grimaces, sneers, and anxious grins. A century later, the work of Hermenegildo Bustos, a nineteenth-century chronicler of small-town personalities. His work was beloved of the Mexican poet Octavio Paz, who wrote about the artist for FMR.

Lastly, sculpture by Adolfo Wildt of Milan, a latter-day alchemist of marble, who worked mainly in the first third of the twentieth century and who transformed base matter into light. Wildt thought his work "should be like a pebble smoothed by running water, though retaining all the planes of its characteristic structure," a structure that corresponded to the human face.

Physiognomies Out of Time

Facing page
Portrait of a Young Woman in Red
Roman period, AD 90–120
Encaustic (wax and pigments) on
limewood, with gold leaf, 15 × 7¼ in
(38.1 × 18.4 cm)
New York, Metropolitan Museum of Art,
Rogers Fund, 1909

Page 98
Portrait of a Man with a Mole on his Nose
Roman period, AD 130–150
Encaustic on limewood, 15½ × 7⅝ in
(39.4 × 19.3 cm)
New York, Metropolitan Museum of Art,
Rogers Fund, 1909
The man is shown turning three-quarters
to the right as he directs his arresting gaze
toward the viewer. His enormous eyes have
highlights and are emphasized by pink
paint along the lids. Pink was also used
to shade the long nose.

Page 99
Panel Portrait of a Man
Roman imperial period, late 1st century AD
Encaustic on wood, 15½ × 8 in
(39.4 × 20.5 cm)
Baltimore, Walters Art Gallery
The young man wears a white cloak and
chiton. His dark skin, highlighted by bright
touches, suggests a typical member of the
mixed Greco-Egyptian population; his
features appear to have been idealized.

Page 100
Head of a Woman, *AD 130–160*
Encaustic with gilded stucco on wood
panel, 17⅝ × 9¾ in (44.8 × 24.8 cm)
Detroit Institute of Art, Gift of Julius H. Haass
This female portrait is enriched by a
heavy gilded stucco relief necklace; her
hairstyle appears to be a variation of the
fashion during Hadrian's reign (AD 117–138),
but, based on stylistic considerations,
a dating to the Antonine period seems
more plausible.

Page 101
Portrait of a Young Woman with
a Gilded Wreath
Roman period, AD 120–40
Encaustic on wood with gold leaf,
14⅜ × 7 in (36.5 × 17.8 cm)
New York, Metropolitan Museum of Art,
Rogers Fund, 1909

The woman's oval face, large eyes,
and slightly open lips give the portrait
considerable presence. The hairstyle is
typical of the reign of Emperor Hadrian
(AD 117–38), except for the corkscrew locks
around the forehead.

The Faces that Were Rome

Page 102
Nero
Emperor AD 54–68
Bronze from Asia Minor, ca. AD 60
Paris, Musée du Louvre, Département des
Antiquités Grecques, Étrusques et Romaines
The son of Agrippina the Younger's first
husband, Nero was adopted by Claudius,
who had married his mother and gave
him his daughter Claudia Octavia as
a wife. Nero later repudiated her to marry
Poppaea and subsequently Messalina. He
was the last emperor of the Julio-Claudian
dynasty.

Page 103
Hadrian
Emperor AD 117–38
Bronze from Egypt, AD 120–30
Paris, Musée du Louvre, Département des
Antiquités Grecques, Étrusques et Romaines
Hadrian became emperor through adoption
by Trajan.

Pages 104–105
Theatrical mask, *detail of the Dionysiac*
frieze, 70–60 BC
Fresco
Pompeii, Villa of Mysteries, Room of the
Great Painting

The Art of Gandhara

Page 106
Maitreya Sitting in the Lotus Position
Northern Pakistan, 2nd/3rd century AD
Schist
Rome, Museo delle Civiltà

Page 107
Princely Head
Pakistan or Afghanistan, 4th century AD
Painted stucco
Rome, Museo delle Civiltà

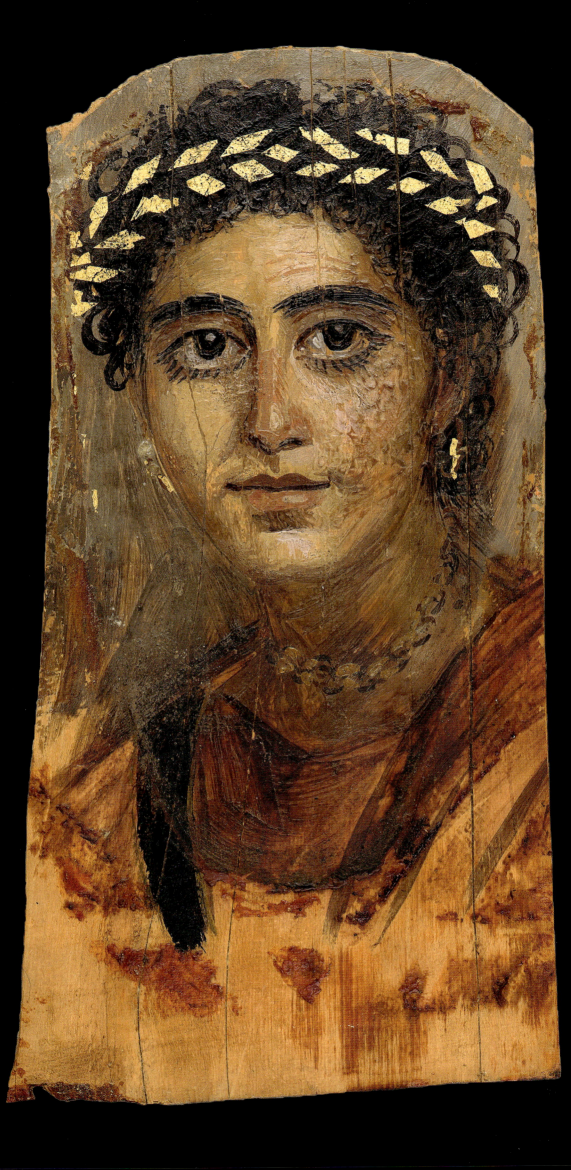

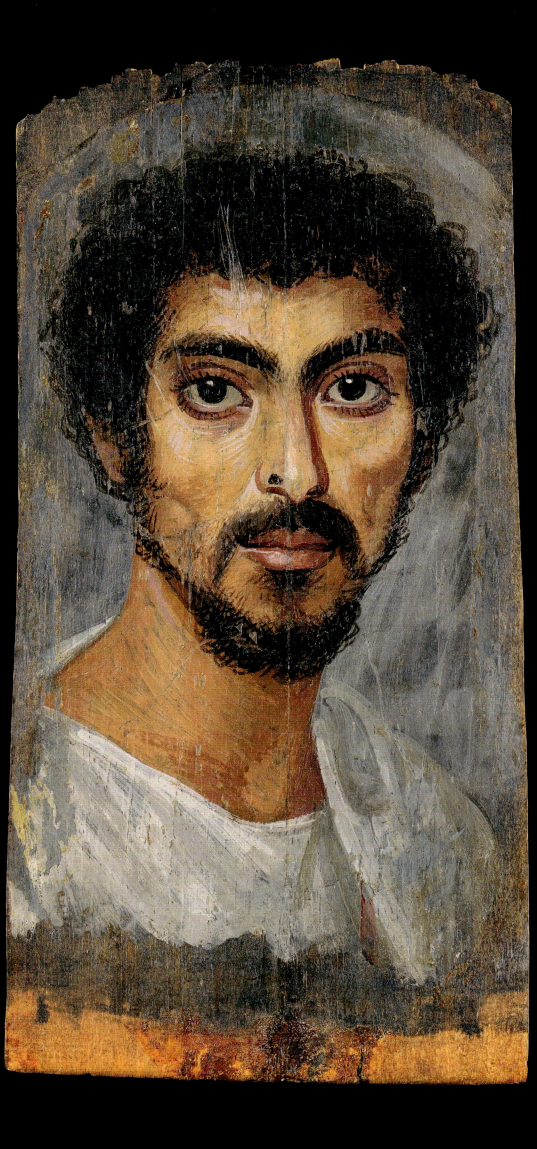

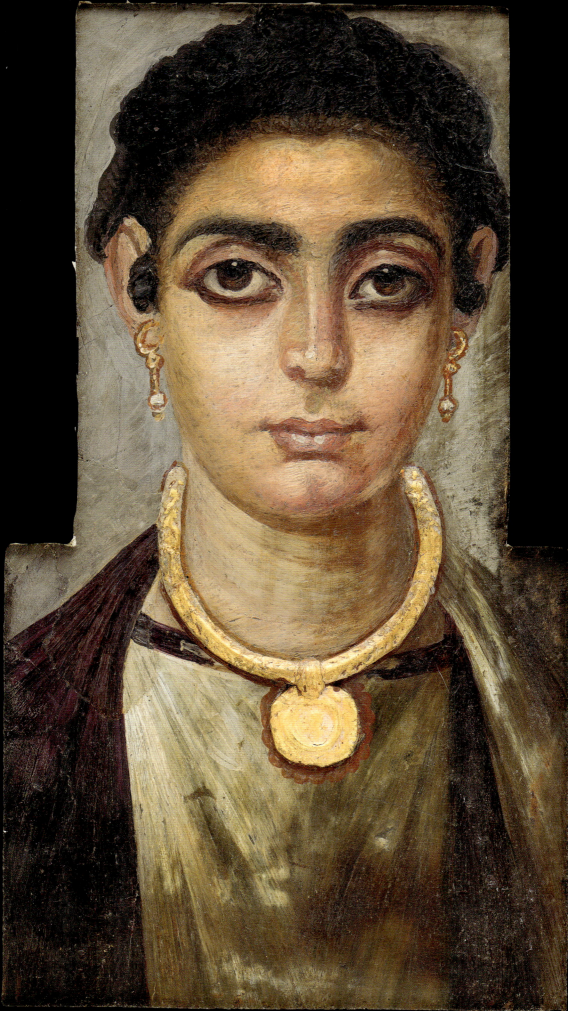

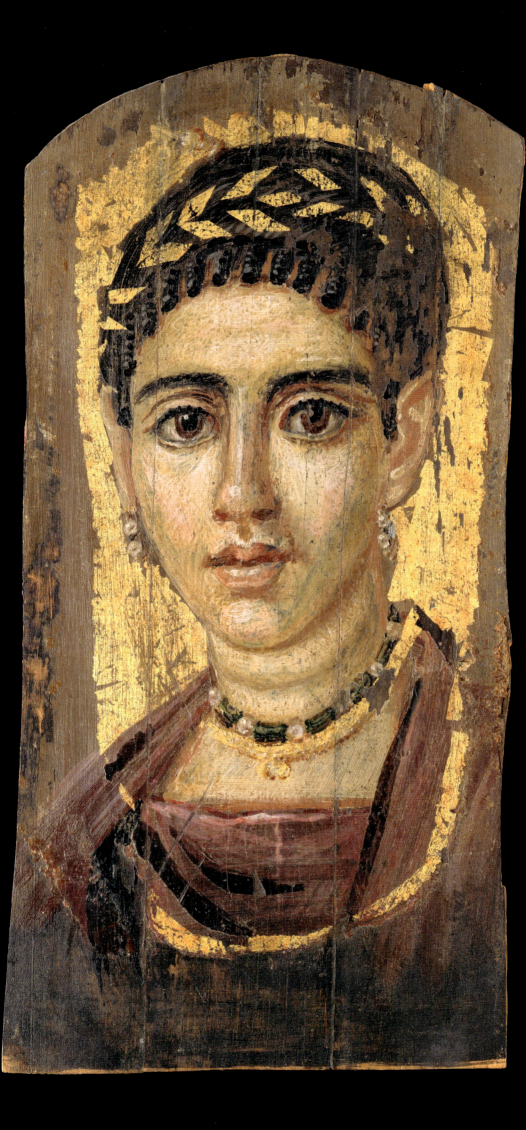

Courtly Visage

Facing page
Giovanna Garzoni (1600–1670)
Catherine of Austria, Duchess of Savoy *(?)*,
signed
Oil on wood, 17⅜ × 12⅞ in (44 × 33 cm)
Florence, Uffizi Gallery

*It is not known for certain whether the
subject of this portrait is the mother or
the wife (Christine) of Victor Amadeus I.
In the "Fatture che io Giovanna Garzoni
presentai al S.mo Gran Ducha" (the artist's
Piedmontese invoices), there is mention of
a "head copied from real life of the Infanta
Catherine of Savoy."*

Pages 110–11
*Alessandro Bonvicino, known as Moretto
da Brescia (ca. 1492–1554)*
Portrait of a Young Gentleman, *1535–40*
*Oil on canvas, 44⅞ × 37⅛ in
(114 × 94.4 cm)*
London, National Gallery

*This lavishly dressed sitter, wearing a
coat lined with lynx or snow-leopard
fur, is probably the Brescian nobleman
and humanist Fortunato Martinengo.
His pose, with his head resting on his
hand, is associated with melancholy.
The inscription in Greek on his cap
means: "Alas, I yearn too much." It is
unclear whether he longs for knowledge,
for some person, or for a pilgrimage.*

Household with Infante

Pages 112 and 113
Francisco Goya (1746–1828)
The Family of the Infante Don Luis
de Borbón, *1783*
Oil on canvas, 97⅝ × 130 in (248 × 330 cm)
Parma, Fondazione Magnani-Rocca

Details of the Portrait of the Infante
Don Luis de Borbón *and the* Infante's Wife,
María Teresa Vallabriga

Pages 114–15
Francisco Goya
The Family of the Infante Don Luis
de Borbón, *1783*
Oil on canvas, 97⅝ × 130 in (248 × 330 cm)
Parma, Fondazione Magnani-Rocca

Detail of the imposing figures of Don
Manuel Moreno, *head of the Infante's
secretariat;* Don Gregorio Ruiz de Arce,
chamber assistant; and Don Alejandro
de la Cruz, *court painter to His Highness.*

A Grimace in Time

Pages 116–19
Franz Xaver Messerschmidt (1736–1783)
Dandy Crossed in Love
Plaster, height 16 in (41 cm)
An Intentional Buffoon
Alabaster and plaster, height 16 in (41 cm)
The Malevolent Man *(detail)*
Tin and lead alloy, height 15⅛ in (38.5 cm)
The Hanged Man
Reddish alabaster, height 15 in (38 cm)
Vienna, Österreichische Galerie Belvedere

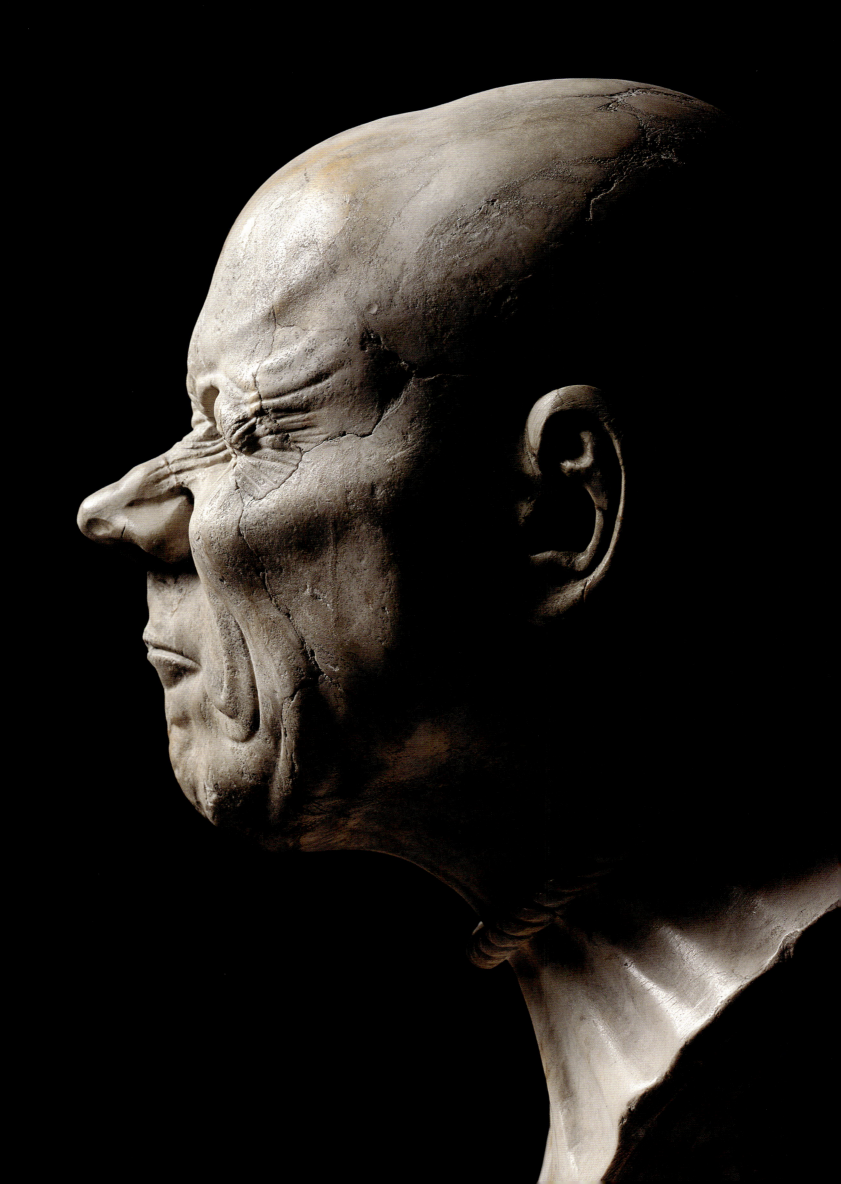

Registrar of His Pueblo

Facing page
Hermenegildo Bustos (1832–1907)
Francisca Valdivia, 1856
Oil on metal, 9¾ × 7 in (24.8 × 17.7 cm)
Private Collection

Pages 122 and 123, left to right
Hermenegildo Bustos
José María Aranda, 1864
Oil on canvas, 16⅛ × 11⅜ in (41 × 29 cm)

Hermenegildo Bustos
Juanita Quesada, 1864
Oil on canvas, 16⅛ × 11⅝ in (41 × 29.5 cm)
Ahondiga Collection

Hermenegildo Bustos
Secundino Gutiérrez, 1864
Oil on metal, 13⅜ × 9½ in (34 × 24 cm)
INBA Collection

Hermenegildo Bustos
Señora con Mantón, 1861
Oil on canvas, 25¾ × 19½ in
(65.5 × 49.5 cm)
Guanajuato, Museo de l'Alhóndiga de
Granaditas, INAH

Pages 124–25
Hermenegildo Bustos
Wedding Portrait, 1883
Oil on canvas, 55.5 × 72.5 cm)
INBA Collection

Magician of Marble

Page 93
Adolfo Wildt (1868–1931)
Thread of Gold, 1927
Marble, height 13¾ in (35 cm)
Private Collection

Pages 126–27
Adolfo Wildt
Vir Temporis Acti, ca. 1911
Carrara marble, height 29⅛ in (74 cm)
Masone Labyrinth, Franco Maria
Ricci Collection

Page 128
Adolfo Wildt
St. Francis, 1929
Marble, height 17¾ in (45 cm)
Forlì, Museo Civico

Page 129
Adolfo Wildt
A Rosary, 1915
Marble with gilt on the braid,
height 16½ in (42 cm)
Private Collection

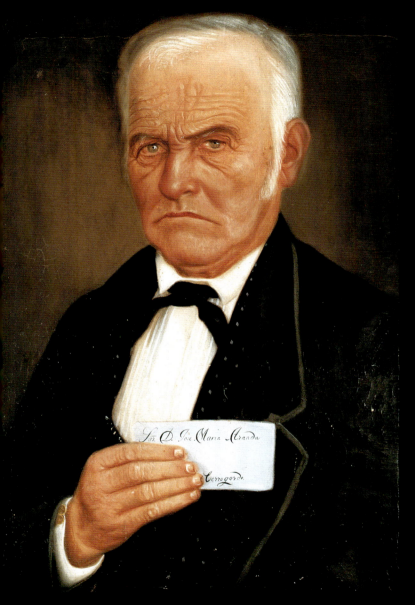

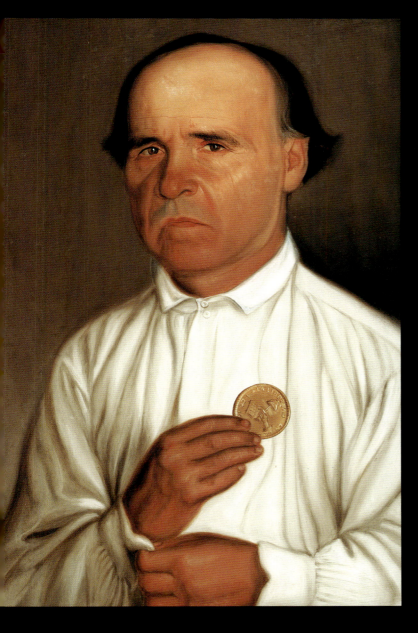

East Meets West Meets East

Galileo and the King of Siam
The Alhambra of Tuscany
Maestro to the Kangxi Emperor

In issue no. 4 of the Italian edition of FMR, from June 1982, the lead article was titled "Alhambra Anastatica." This was taken from a term meaning "facsimile of the Alhambra," which reflects a certain ideological bent, wrapped up with the fact that Ricci himself had undertaken a number of heroic facsimile editions. The anastatic Alhambra in question was an Orientalist dream, a Moorish castle in the countryside just outside of Florence. Sadly, it now seems to be heading for collapse and rubble.

Almost as if every detail of every article in FMR's extensive history recapitulated the qualities and ambitions of the enterprise at large, the very word "anastatic" reveals significant forebears. Indeed, on April 12, 1845, an article by Edgar Allan Poe appeared in the *Broadway Journal* under the headline "Anastatic Printing." Remarking on this new invention, Poe seems to be echoing the spirit with which we greet AI today: "By means of this discovery anything written, drawn, or printed, can be made to stereotype itself, with absolute accuracy, in five minutes." As a consequence, "The wealthy gentleman of elegant leisure will lose the vantage-ground now afforded him, and will be forced to tilt on terms of equality with the poor devil author."

Indeed, the palace of Sammezzano was the creation of a man obsessed: Ferdinando Panciatichi Ximenes d'Aragona spent almost forty years working on this astounding reproduction of the Alhambra. The building has generated its own legends. Although it is in fact a very substantial sixty-room mansion, it is often said to contain a room for every day of the year, much like the grim country estate of Malplaquet in T. H. White's novel *Mistress Masham's Repose* (1946), which had 365 windows, "all broken but six." Malplaquet also boasted "Vistas, Obelisks, Pyramids, Columns, Temples, Rotundas, and Palladian Bridges," to say nothing of the crowning glory, a lake called the Quincunx with a small overgrown island possessing the folly that gave the book its name: "a plastered temple in the shape of a cupola, or rather, to give it its proper name, a monopteron. It was a dome like the top of an eggshell, raised on five slender columns."

White comments on "dainty elegance…abandoned in the March of Mind." Poe, writing about anastatic printing but commenting on the world and its ways, quoted the philosopher Francis Bacon: "There is no exquisite beauty without some strangeness in the proportions." That might be an epigram for FMR.

The introduction to the article on Sammezzano told the story succinctly: "In the mid-nineteenth century, a Tuscan gentleman set out to reproduce the Alhambra on his vast estate. Mosaics, tiles, patterns of colored glass, exotic columns, stalactites covered with tiny mirrors—detail by detail he transformed his villa into an improbable Moorish palace. Testimony to an artistic vision or a dreamer's folly? Sammezzano is eerie in its ghostlessness, depressing in its repetition, fascinating in its insignificance."

Very much in keeping with FMR's charter of lost causes, forgotten kingdoms, unreasonable ambitions, and magical thinking, is it any surprise that the two other topics treated here are a spectacular public palace built by a Tuscan architect and painter for the King of Siam in the late nineteenth century, and a Milan-born Jesuit missionary who went to China in 1715 and stayed for fifty years, becoming court painter to the Kangxi Emperor? The truth: so often stranger than fiction.

Galileo and the King of Siam

Page 135
Galileo Chini (1873–1956)
Nostalgic Hour on the Me-Nam River,
1912–13
Oil on canvas, 49 × 49 in
(124.4 × 124.4 cm)
Tortona, "Il Divisionismo" Pinacoteca
Fondazione Cassa di Risparmio di Tortona

Pages 136–39
Galileo Chini
Decoration of the Throne Room of Siam,
Bangkok, 1911–13

Pages 140–41
Galileo Chini
The Festival of the Last Day of the Chinese
Year in Bangkok, 1912–13
Oil on canvas, 120 × 126 in (305 × 320 cm)
Florence, Galleria Nazionale d'Arte
Moderna, Palazzo Pitti

The Alhambra of Tuscany

Pages 142 and 143
Sammezzano, decorative details
Reggello, Florence

Pages 144–45
Hall of the Peacocks, *Sammezzano*

This hall is named after the polychrome
stucco voussoirs that resemble peacock tails.
Note the marble baseboard, the ceramic-tile
wainscoting, the painted stucco columns,
and the terracotta floor.

Pages 146 and 147
Sammezzano, decorative details

Pages 148–49
Hall of Lovers, *Sammezzano*

As its name suggests, this hall is a shrine
to the most renowned lovers of chivalric
literature. It is entirely covered with white
stucco scrollwork and floral motifs. On the
wall of the entryway and the facing wall,
one can read in gilded letters the names
of Clorinda, Tancred, Erminia, Rinaldo,
Armida, Lancelot, Guinevere, Bradamante,
Orlando, Angelica, Medoro, Tristan,
and Iseult (Isolde).

Maestro to the Kangxi Emperor

Giuseppe Castiglione was born in 1688 in Milan; as a young Jesuit brother, he painted canvases in oils in the transitional style of the time, mixing late Baroque and the dawning Rococo style. Almost eighty years later, he died in Beijing with the name Lang Shih-Ning and the rank of Mandarin, Second to the Kangxi Emperor. Castiglione left a remarkable body of work: paintings on silk of emperors, concubines, flowers, countless animals, and especially horses, symbols to the Manchu ruling class of a long-lost nomadic freedom.

Facing page
Giuseppe Castiglione (1688–1766)
Portrait of the Qianlong Emperor
on Horseback
*Vertical silk scroll, 126¾ × 130¾ in
(322 × 332 cm)*
Beijing, The Palace Museum

Page 152
Giuseppe Castiglione
Official Portrait of the Qianlong Emperor
in Court Garb
*Vertical silk scroll, 95¼ × 70½ in
(242 × 179 cm)*
Beijing, The Palace Museum

Page 153
Giuseppe Castiglione
Portrait of Empress Xiaoxian Chun
*Vertical silk scroll, 95¼ × 70½ in
(242 × 179 cm)*
Beijing, The Palace Museum

Pages 154–55
Giuseppe Castiglione
One Hundred Horses Scroll
Silk scroll, 37¼ × 307 in (94.5 × 780 cm)
Taipei, National Palace Museum

Page 156
Giuseppe Castiglione
One of the Ten Prized Dogs
*Vertical silk scroll, 97½ × 64½ in
(247.5 × 163.7 cm)*
Taipei, National Palace Museum

Page 157
Giuseppe Castiglione
Cochin Lemur
*Ink and pigment on vertical silk scroll,
43¼ × 33⅜ in (109.8 × 84.7 cm)*
Taipei, National Palace Museum

純惠皇貴妃

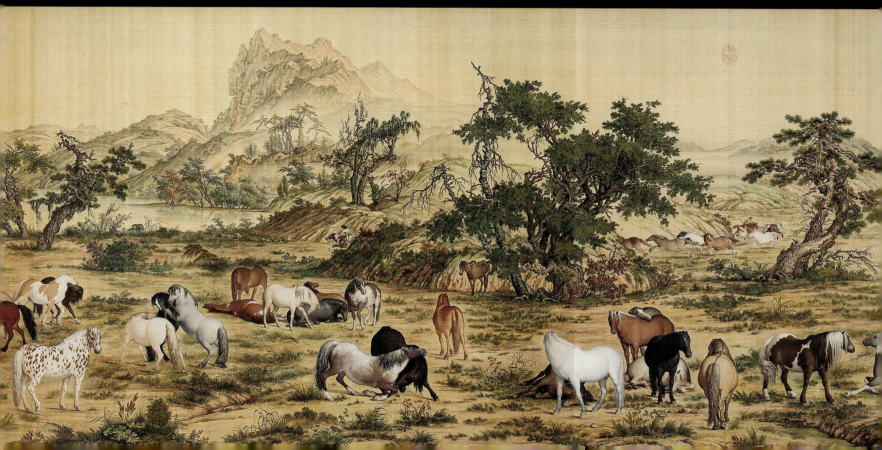

寓屬生交阯自
呼名果然歡同
難還共小浚大
居前柳異王孫
惡郭齋君子賢
不因皮適褥林
霙命寧捐

御題交阯果然詩
臣于敏中奉

勒敬書

A Hard Metallic Sheen

Sharp and Shining
Under the Volcano
Reliquarian to the Saints
Armor Makes the Man

In Sir Thomas Malory's *Le Morte d'Arthur* (1485), Lancelot is brought by clamoring townsfolk to a fair tower to rescue a lady imprisoned therein. Even though Gawain himself had already despaired of saving her, Lancelot, nothing daunted, boldly went in and there "took the fairest lady by the hand that ever he saw, and she was naked as a needle." Naked as a needle: that lovely expression from pre-industrial times points to the immense impression something as sharp and shiny as a needle must have made in a world of dirt and rough surfaces. A needle, gleaming and alternately hidden and revealed, feminine in nature, yet biting and capable of drawing blood.

In the seaside town of Ravenna stands the so-called Mausoleum of Galla Placidia, named for a woman who served briefly as both regent and empress consort of the Roman empire. Although the building is no larger than a comfortable apartment, it was adorned with luminous mosaics around AD 425, a thousand years and more before Malory compared the sheen of a needle to naked skin. Those hard glass tiles, or *tesserae*, glowing with gold and cobalt and green, depict scenes of Heaven, including two Christological doves on the rim of a birdbath. Mosaics, after all, are able to evoke both brilliant sunshine and night skies.

The art professor who introduced me to the art of late antiquity, Pietro Scarpellini, mused while showing a slide of that scene: "Try to imagine what seeing this meant to a shepherd almost 2,000 years ago, eh? He'd never seen a painting, much less a glistening mosaic, in his life. He thought he was looking at Paradise."

In the game of gold and brushes that artists have played over the centuries and the millennia, there is nothing quite as magical as the hard metallic sheen of enamel, metal, mosaic, pearl, and cloisonné. Reflective surfaces and dimensionless sheen are everywhere in our modern world, but they were a hypnotic, once-in-a-lifetime impression in an era when art belonged to the great and the powerful. It wasn't just rustic shepherds who could be astonished by the sight of mosaic doves in the empyrean. The American songwriter Cole Porter is said to have been inspired by his visit to the Mausoleum of Galla Placidia to write the meltingly romantic jazz classic "Night and Day." That was in the 1920s, fifteen centuries after the mosaicist put down his tools, yet Porter was deeply moved by those artificial glass skies: "Night and day, you are the one./ Only you beneath the moon and under the sun."

We've selected six fine examples of how the sheen might have been experienced in bygone centuries—and in the present day. Bronze busts from Herculaneum, covered over by the same eruption in AD 79 that buried Pompeii, preserving it for posterity; reliquaries made of silver, bronze, copper, gilt bronze, precious stones, and pearls; German jousting armor from the sixteenth century; the bodywork and radiator-cap sculptures crafted in the 1920s by Ettore Bugatti, for cars that Porter may well have ridden in; the gilt-bronze statuary of two imperial families, those of Charles V and Philip II, in Spain's Escorial, a spectacular three-dimensional rendering of two of the most powerful families on Earth in their day; and finally, the metallic thread and yarn tapestries of Olga de Amaral, a Colombian textile artist, whom FMR dubbed "the Penelope of the Andes."

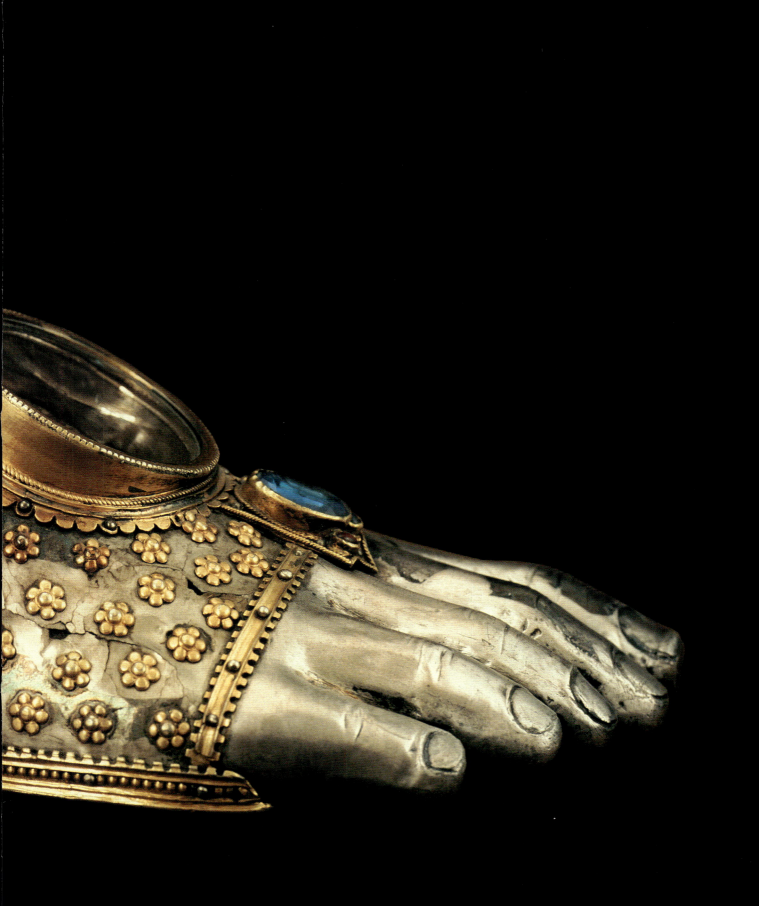

Armor Makes the Man

Facing page
Helmet with mask-style visor *from a*
suit of fluted jousting armor belonging to
Duke Ulrich of Württemberg (1487–1550)
Made by the armorer Wilhelm von Worms
the Elder
Nuremberg, ca. 1525–50
Vienna, Kunsthistorisches Museum
Ulrich of Württemberg fought beside
Maximilian I in the expeditions of 1508
against Venice, and in 1513 against
Burgundy. After the Swabian League drove
him out of his duchy, he went over to the
side of the reformers and became a fierce
enemy of the Habsburgs.

Pages 176 and 177
Helmet with mask-type visor *from a suit*
of fluted jousting armor belonging to
the mercenary leader Wolf Dietrich von
Hohenems (1507–1538)
Southern Germany, ca. 1525–30
Vienna, Kunsthistorisches Museum
Wolf Dietrich von Hohenems fought at
the battle of Pavia in 1525 in the service
of King Charles V.

Pages 178 and 179
Helmet with visor *in the form of a grotesque*
mask from a suit of "parade" armor
belonging to Albrecht of Brandenburg,
Duke of Prussia (1491–1568)
Possibly Braunschweig, ca. 1526
Vienna, Kunsthistorisches Museum
Albrecht of Brandenburg was a grand
master of the Order of the Teutonic Knights.
In 1526, he married Dorothy of Denmark
and secularized the territory of the Order
in eastern Prussia, thus becoming the first
Duke of Prussia. The newlywed couple
engraved on the back of the helmet indicates
that this suit of armor was ordered for the
occasion of his wedding.

Incomparable Bugatti

Pages 180–81
Type 41 Royale Coupé Napoléon (1926–32)
With this model, in 1926, Bugatti presented
the strongest, largest, and most luxurious
automobile in the world, characterized
by unimaginable power and opulent
equipment. The first prototype was built
in 1926, but it was based on a longer
wheelbase and a larger engine with a
displacement of 14.7 litres. It wasn't until
1932 that Bugatti sold the first Royale,
to the Parisian industrialist Armand Esders.
An elegant roadster body by Jean Bugatti
sheathed the eight-cylinder above the
drive. In this car, which was just under
20 ft (about 6 m) long, the passenger
communicated with the driver via an
electric intercom. The Royale is the only
Bugatti vehicle to have a hood ornament.
It features a dancing elephant, designed
by Ettore's deceased brother Rembrandt
Bugatti, a well-known artist and sculptor.

Pages 182–83
Front of the Type 57 (1937–40)
Eight cylinders, 3,257 cc. displacement
Mulhouse, Musée National de l'Automobile

Pages 184–85
Bugatti Type 35B Sport, US Coachwork, 1927
Mulhouse, Musée National de l'Automobile
The two-seater is considered to be the car
that marked a "turning point," pioneering
the concept of a holistically conceived,
race-ready car available for purchase.
This extraordinarily successful car won
more than 1,000 races in its time.

Pages 186–87
Type 57SC Coupé Atlantic
Mulhouse, Musée National de l'Automobile
The Atlantic is often said to be the first
supercar. In common with the other models
in the Type 57 series, it was equipped with
an inline eight engine with a displacement
of 3,257 cc, which, when supercharged
with a Roots-type compressor, propelled
it to a top speed of 130 mph (210 km/h)—
exceptionally fast for its time. It is also
considered the third most expensive car
in the world, following the Ferrari 250
GTO and the Mercedes-Benz 300 SLR
Uhlenhaut; chassis no. 57734, built in 1936
for the banker Victor Rothschild and now
housed at the Mullin Automotive Museum,
California, was reportedly sold at auction in
2010 for more than $30 million.

Pages 188–89
Type 101 Cabriolet, Coachwork Gangloff
Mulhouse, Musée National de l'Automobile

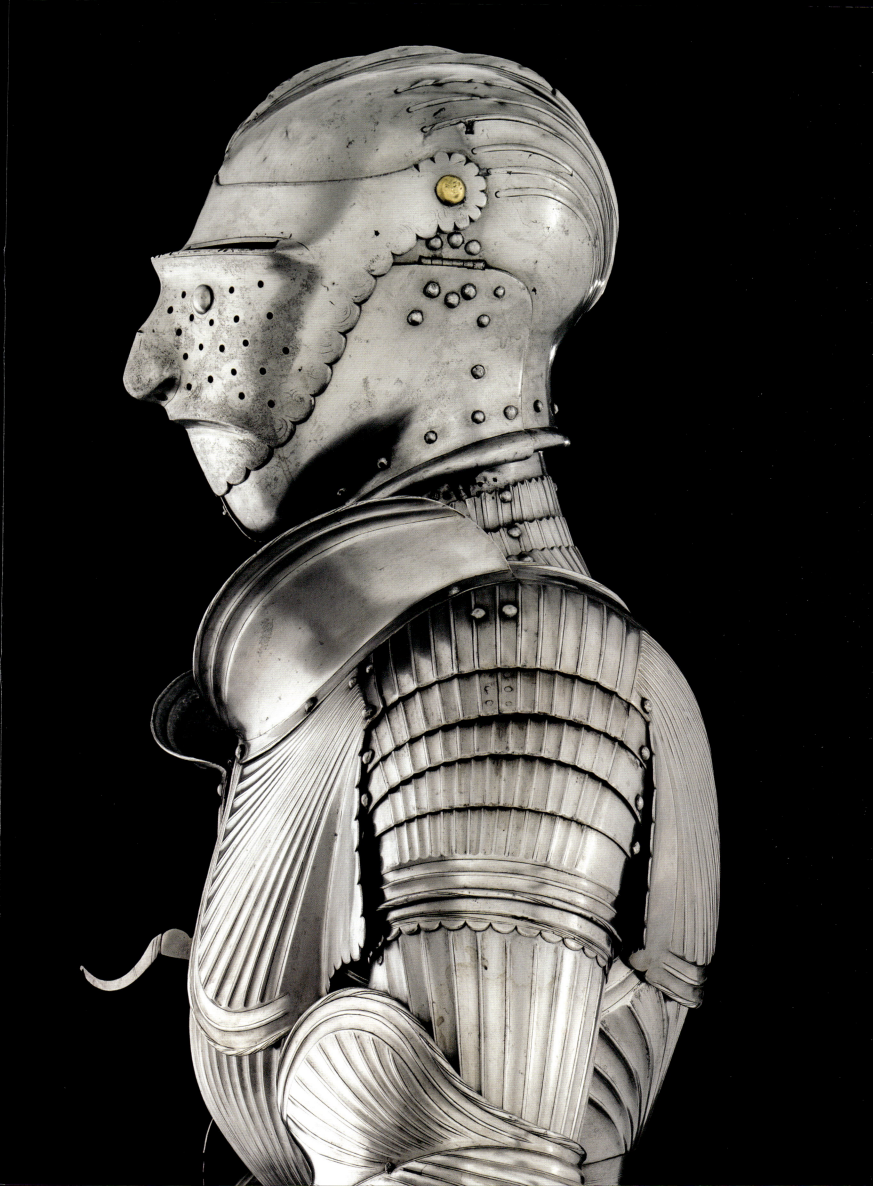

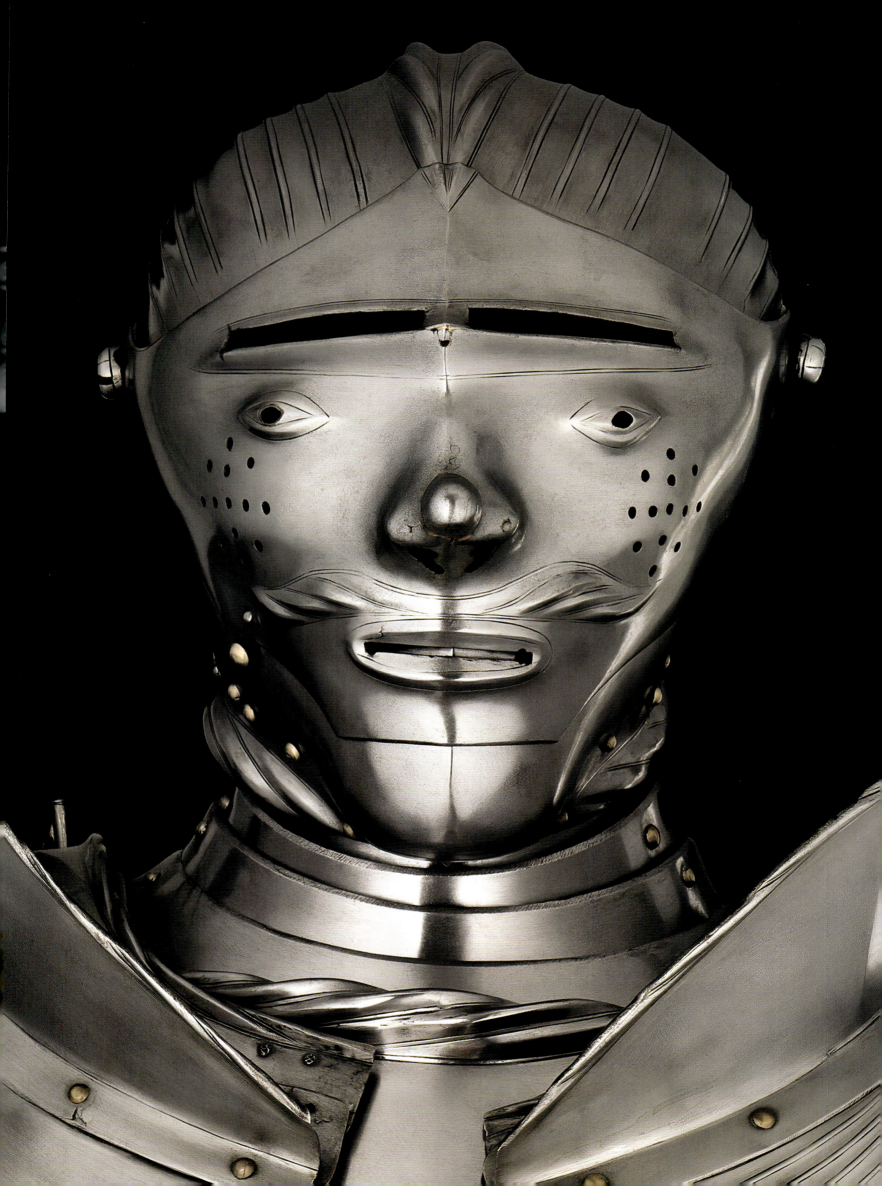

At Prayer for Eternity

*Pages 191 (detail of Empress Isabella),
192, and 194–95
Pompeo Leoni (1533–1608)
Tomb of Emperor Charles V, 1592–97
Gilt bronze, jasper, and polychrome marble
San Lorenzo de El Escorial*

*The praying group includes, besides
the emperor, his wife, Empress Isabella
of Portugal; his sisters Mary, Queen of
Hungary, and Eleanor, Queen of France;
and his daughter Mary, Empress of
Germany.*

*Page 193
Pompeo Leoni
Tomb of Philip II, 1600–1601
Gilt bronze, jasper, and polychrome marble
San Lorenzo de El Escorial*

*As well as the king, the group includes three
of his four wives (Anna of Austria, Elisabeth
of Valois, and Mary of Portugal) and his son
Prince Charles.*

The Penelope of the Andes

*Pages 196–97
Olga de Amaral (born 1932)
Foreground: Estelas 57 (diptych), 48
Background: Estelas 52, 67, 62, 54, 53, 50
Collection of the artist*

*Page 198
Olga de Amaral
Montaña 38, 2014
Linen, gesso, acrylic pigments, gold leaf,
silver, and palladium, 39¾ × 47¼ in
(100 × 120 cm)
Collection of the artist*

*Page 199
Olga de Amaral
Umbra 59, 2014
Linen, gesso, acrylic pigments, and
gold leaf, 78¾ × 47¼ in (200 × 120 cm)
Collection of the artist*

PHIL II

IVENT SIMVI   A VXOR
ET MARIA H   ATRICES
LLONORA L   RORES
ILAFRANC H   REGINÆ

QVI
ELISAB
CVM C
VL ANNA
RIA VXORES
FIL·PRIMOG·

Playthings of the Great and Small

Children and play are a recurring motif in the universal world of art. They are, of course, strangely adult when the time comes for their close-up, seemingly the less childish the further back in time the depiction. Perhaps that's because children faced such a harrowing path in those darker days, or perhaps because we overlay our own anxieties in *these* darker days. As the writer G. K. Chesterton put it: "Fairy tales do not tell children that dragons exist. Children already know that dragons exist. Fairy tales tell children the dragons can be killed."

There are a surprising number of children at play in the pages of FMR, and as many if not more adults at play, as well. Those, however, are only the denizens of the painted or sculpted—or, in any case, depicted—worlds. The artists themselves are, by inclination, playful, so a selection of art about playfulness becomes a sort of *mise en abyme*, a double-mirroring effect of like within like, story within story, children acting older than their age and adults acting younger.

Paradoxically, the most precious objects here are the ones at greatest risk: rattles for teething infants, although their state of conservation suggests that they spent relatively little time in the hands of their ostensibly intended recipients. Sturdier and much likelier to have received hard use are mechanical piggy banks, mementos of an era of cast iron and brightly colored enamels. Then we have the two great diametrically opposed interfaces with reality: chess and slot machines. The first contains a world of rational strategy, the second a universe of irrational hope of reward and a coin-fed door to the grim contingency of impoverishment.

Herodotus tells us that games in general were invented in the midst of famine, to *distract* the populace from grim contingencies. Chess, by contrast, seems to partake of reality to an almost spasmodic degree. It is a Platonic ideal of warfare: bloodless, unhurried, but ruthless nonetheless. The boards can be unrivaled works of marquetry, made of ebony, mahogany, ivory, or amber. Slot machines embody a different interface with reality; if chess is about focus and attention, slot machines are about distraction and addiction. To paraphrase from the introductory paragraph of the magazine article: "There are giant slot machines and dwarf machines, machines both skinny and obese, machines that are lopsided and off-kilter; machines that are sleek and rectangular. They can be made of wood, brightly painted cast-iron, or polished chrome. Some are vulgar and simple to a fault, others, far more elegant, boast Art Nouveau motifs: highly stylized horns of plenty. To slip a coin into the slot is to bargain with an influx of uncertainty: Can I hope for two cherries and a lemon?"

Finally, the games of the sophisticated and mature: the *villeggiatura* (holiday pastimes) of country estates in the early eighteenth-century work of Antonio Visentini; riding to hounds in a painting by George Stubbs a little later in the same century; and posters for British golf courses produced by local railroad companies in the 1930s.

Portrait of the Aristocrat

Facing page
Pietro Melchiorre Ferrari (1734/35–1787)
Portrait of Antonio Ghidini with His Family
(detail), after 1769
Oil on canvas
Fontanellato, Masone Labyrinth,
Franco Maria Ricci Collection

Proud of his happy family, Antonio Ghidini invited one of Parma's finest artists to depict them all in a strikingly natural composition, appearing to capture a moment of domestic intimacy, in keeping with the then new direction of English art, the "conversation piece." The painting can be dated to 1769 or later through the portrait medallion held by the boy in the blue headdress. It commemorates the wedding in 1769 of Maria Amalia of Habsburg and Ferdinand of Bourbon.

Page 206
Giuseppe Duprà (1703–1784)
Portrait of Charles Felix, son of Victor
Amadeus III of Savoy and Maria Antonia
Ferdinanda of Spain, 1762–67
Oil on canvas, 43 × 34½ in (109 × 87.4 cm)
Turin, Stupinigi, Hunting Lodge

Born in Turin in 1765, Charles Felix was the Duke of Genoa and, from 1814 to 1821, Viceroy of Sardinia. He unwillingly took the throne that same year, and restored absolutist rule with Austrian support. In 1807, he married Maria Christina of Bourbon, the daughter of Ferdinand IV of Naples, king now of Sicily alone. Charles Felix died without issue in 1831, and the succession passed to the cadet branch of the House of Savoy, in the person of Charles Albert of Carignano.

Page 207
Giuseppe Duprà
Portrait of Victor Emmanuel I, son of Victor
Amadeus III of Savoy and Maria Antonia
Ferdinanda of Spain, 1762–67
Oil on canvas, 42½ × 34½ in (108 × 87.5 cm)
Turin, Stupinigi, Hunting Lodge

Born in 1759, Victor Emmanuel I took the title of Duke of Aosta. In 1789, he married Maria Theresa of Habsburg-Lorraine, daughter of Archduke Ferdinand; she bore him six children. From 1792 to 1796, he led Piedmontese troops against France. Forced to flee to Sardinia with the entire royal family, he took the throne upon his brother's abdication. When Napoleon fell from power in 1814, Victor Emmanuel

regained his mainland possessions, with the welcome addition of Liguria. He worked to restore the ancien régime, enabling reactionary courtiers in a reign of ludicrous excess and savagery. In 1821, in the face of a revolt by army officers, he chose to abdicate in favor of his brother Charles Felix. He died shortly afterward.

Rattles of Ivory and Coral

Page 208
Two 19th-century rattles. Left, a silver-gilt model embossed with floral motifs, reminiscent of English corals; right, a French-inspired model decorated with a floral motif on the medallion.

Page 209
Two 19th-century silver rattles with ivory handles; the shafts are decorated with a shell and a revolving ball.

Page 210
Two 19th-century silver rattles; the one on the left has an embossed and chased medallion decorated with a little Cupid playing a pipe, a self-referential allusion to the object's use; the one on the right has an ivory handle and its shaft is decorated with a turret.

Page 211
An 18th-century silver rattle with double row of brackets, twisted shaft, and whistle with mascaron; the handle has been lost.
All at Santa Maria del Piano, Parma, Mario Lanfranchi Collection

Unbreakable Banks

Page 212
Sprite Boy penny bank
United States, ca. 1960
Cast iron, height 7 in (18 cm)

Page 213
Speaking Dog penny bank
United States, 1940–50
Cast iron, height 7½ in (19 cm)

Pages 214–15
Russell A. Frisbie (creator), J. & E. Stevens Co. (producer)
William Tell mechanical money box, late 19th–early 20th century
Cast iron, height 4¾ in (12 cm)
All: Turin, Museo del Risparmio

Infinity in a Chessboard

Page 201
Chess Players, carved mirror valve, ca. 1300
Ivory
Paris, Musée du Louvre

Facing page
Sofonisba Anguissola (1532–1625)
The Game of Chess (detail), 1555
Oil on canvas
Poznan, National Museum

The young artist chose the subject of chess because she and all her sisters played. The game was widespread at the time, and it was considered an excellent intellectual exercise for women, while card games and dice were forbidden to them. It should be noted, however, that the board is placed incorrectly: that is, with the black and not the white player's square at the bottom right. An error, although at the time the position of the chessboard was not definitively established.

Pages 218 and 219
Portable box for games of chess and trictrac in wood and ivory, 15th century
Private Collection

This box is of Andalusian manufacture, its floral inlays and geometric decorations inspired by Islamic motifs. The cultural importance of chess in history and art history has made it the noblest of games, one of the few to survive since earliest antiquity.

Pages 220 and 221
Made in Prussia, perhaps in Königsberg (now Kaliningrad) in the workshop of Georg Schreiber (ca. 1600), this exceptional game board documents the prevalence of fossil resin in Wunderkammer pieces along the Baltic Sea. An example is the renowned Amber Room, removed from Berlin's Charlottenburg Castle and donated in 1716 by the King of Prussia to his Russian ally Peter the Great.
Private Collection

Pages 222 and 223
Chess pieces
Inlaid and openwork ivory
Private Collection

Both Mughal and Arab culture owed much to Persian culture, which was in turn a bridge between the Mediterranean and Chinese worlds. At the time of the East India Company and, later, the British Raj

in India, many carved chess pieces bore the features of European troops, or in some cases perhaps the diwan *or senior official at courts of rajahs, or even the British monarch. In common with Chinese porcelain, these objects were meant for export. The elephant-ivory chess pieces were made from the tusk's full cross section, generally at tip or base. Some of the pieces therefore had curved, compact shapes.*

Pages 224–25
Cover of a chessboard, Germany, 16th century
Ivory and ebony
Private Collection

The decorations of insects, fruit, and plants are possibly heraldic references.

Enameled Bandits

Page 226
12, 1895
29⅛ × 18⅞ × 7½ in (74 × 48 × 19 cm)
Jean-Claude Baudot Collection

Page 227
Little Duke slot machine
Chicago, Jennings Co., 1931
21⅝ × 13 × 8¼ in (55 × 33 × 21 cm)
Jean-Claude Baudot Collection

Page 228 (left to right, top to bottom)
Électrisez Vous slot machine
France, ca. 1905
20⅞ × 15¾ × 4¾ in (53 × 40 × 12 cm)

The Elk slot machine
Chicago, Mills Novelty Co., 1905
18⅞ × 12½ × 10⅝ in (48 × 32 × 27 cm)

La Comète slot machine
Chicago, Mills Novelty Co., 1906
12½ × 13⅜ × 10⅝ in (32 × 34 × 27 cm)

Tura Bell slot machine
Tura, Germany, 1933
24½ × 16 × 15¾ in (62 × 41 × 40 cm)
All: Jean-Claude Baudot Collection

Page 229
Silent War Eagle slot machine
Chicago, Mills Novelty Co., 1931
25½ × 15¾ × 15 in (65 × 40 × 38 cm)
Jean-Claude Baudot Collection

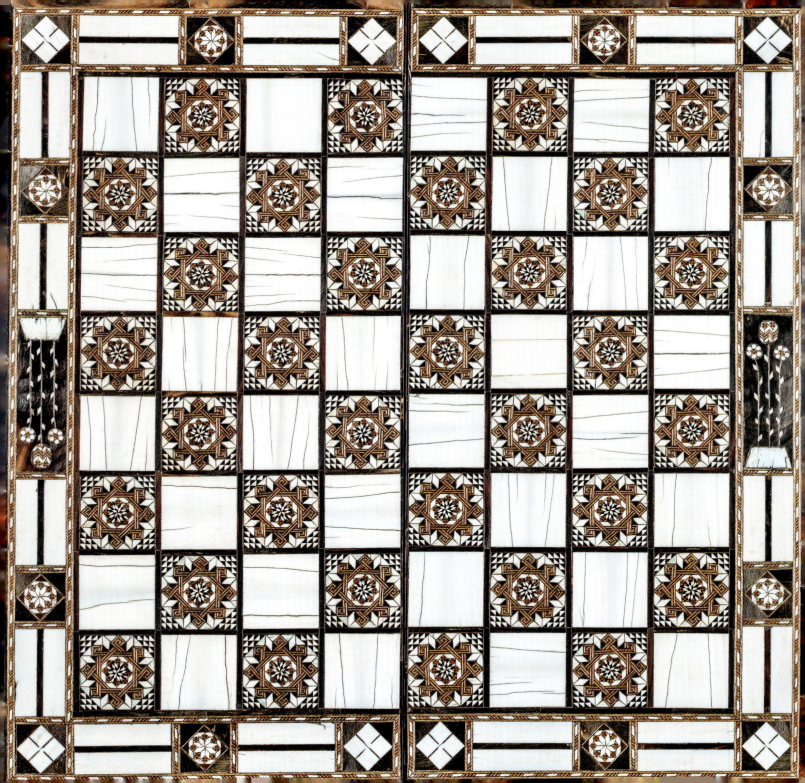

Mise de 1 Franc

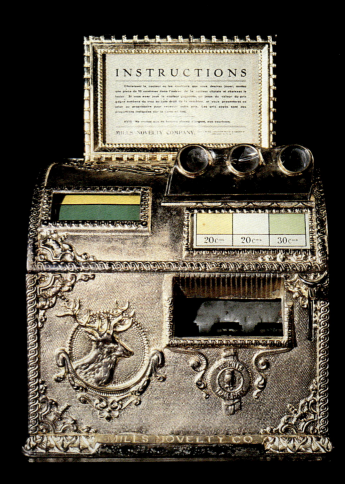

At Play in the Villa

Facing page
Antonio Visentini (1688–1782) and Gaspare
Diziani (1689–1767)
Reading of the Cards (detail). 1739–40
Oil on canvas

Pages 232–33
Antonio Visentini and Gaspare Diziani
Concert in Villa (detail). 1739–40
Oil on canvas

Pages 234–35
Antonio Visentini and Gaspare Diziani
Playing Nine-Pins (detail). 1739–40
Oil on canvas
All: Venice, Palazzo Contarini Fasan

The Thrill of the Chase

Pages 236–37
George Stubbs (1724–1806)
The 3rd Duke of Richmond with the
Charlton Hunt, 1759–60
Oil on canvas, 55 × 97 in (140 × 246 cm)
Surrey, Goodwood Collection
Photograph courtesy of the Trustees

A Good Walk Wasted

Pages 238–39
Then and Now: 600 Golf Courses, London
and North Eastern Railway poster, ca. 1930
York, UK, National Railway Museum

Follies, Visions, Extravaganzas and Deathscapes

The Park of Monsters
Exotic Visions
A Folly in Stone
Giddy Skulls and Bones

G ardens are complicated things: lovely, yet incessant reminders of expulsion from the first garden of them all, Eden. We as a species were evicted and cursed with earning our bread by the sweat of our brow. In gardens there are follies; in dreams lies madness. Take Bomarzo's grove of monsters, the creation of a bullied hunchback duke, Pierfrancesco Orsini—at least, that is how he is portrayed anecdotally, historically, and especially in the novel *Bomarzo* (1962) by Manuel Mujica Láinez. "Every rock had an enigma hidden in its character, and every one of those enigmas was also a secret of my past and my character," the novel's Orsini soliloquizes. He recalls the work of shaping the park: "Only the immovable rocks, placed arbitrarily, preserved their extravagant characteristics in the midst of the civilized expanse, and even they, upon being transformed into strange pieces of sculpture, would take part in that prodigious rediscovery." He speaks of the local stone-carvers, untrained but intuitive, who produced "fantastic rough shapes that brought to the imagination the Etruscan tradition of our soil."

Mujica Láinez portrays Orsini as transported into a trance state midway between artistic rapture and a sorcerer's dark sabbath: "Thick clouds hid the moon and disguised the silhouettes of stones which emerged like strange sails out of the sadness of the valley that had been carved, violated, disemboweled, rough as the waves of a stormy sea. I trembled. I was in a bewitched countryside."

Bomarzo—theatrical and, at half a millennium old, pioneering—is just one of the many remarkable creations of landscape art featured in FMR, theatrical and innovative. The poet Wallace Stevens wrote, "Complacencies of the peignoir, and late/ Coffee and oranges in a sunny chair,/ And the green freedom of a cockatoo/ Upon a rug mingle to dissipate/ The holy hush of ancient sacrifice." Later in the same poem, "Sunday Morning," he writes, "Death is the mother of beauty." Certainly there is a sense of darkness in the extravagant visions that people the pages of FMR, set unerringly against the special black ink that has always distinguished the magazine. Antonio Basoli, for example, was a stage designer and, reportedly, illustrator of spectacular curtains (sadly much, if not most, of his work has been lost). He worked largely in Bologna in the first half of the nineteenth century, and once turned down an offer to work for the composer Gioachino Rossini. Here we feature his spectacular historical vistas of the four corners of Earth and an ancient city. Another visionary obsessive, Tomaso Buzzi, a highly successful architect and interior designer in Milan, retired in 1956 to Umbria, where he bought a thirteenth-century Franciscan convent and transformed it into a dream complex.

Last comes the tradition of the Dance (or Triumph) of Death, which was particularly strong in the fifteenth century, still shaken by the horrors of the Black Death just a century earlier. The bubonic plague slaughtered half of the population of Europe, and that memory haunted the continent's art for many generations to come. Indeed, dancing skeletons are as popular now as ever: an evergreen crowd-pleaser.

The Park of Monsters

Facing page
The Face of Time

Pages 246–47
Statue of a Fury, with Batwings

Page 248
The Leaning House

Page 249
Hercules and Cacus

Pages 250–51
Armida (Sleeping Nymph)

Page 252
The Cavern of the Ages
*Above is L'Orco (The Ogre), the best-
known sculpture from Parco dei Mostri.
The inscription around the mouth reads
"ogni pensiero vola," "every thought flies,"
a reference to the echo inside the cavern,
which is audible from outside.*

Page 253
The Group of Discord
All: Bomarzo, Parco dei Mostri

Exotic Visions

Pages 254–55
Antonio Basoli (1774–1848)
The Four Corners of the World: America,
(detail), 1838
Oil on canvas
Florence, Private Collection

Pages 256–57
Antonio Basoli
The Four Corners of the World: Africa, *1838*
Oil on canvas, 27½ × 34¼ in (70 × 87 cm)
Florence, Private Collection

Pages 258–59
Antonio Basoli
Inner Walls of an Ancient City, *1838*
Oil on canvas, 23⅝ × 31½ in (60 × 80 cm)
Private Collection

A Folly in Stone

Facing page
Façade of the Tower of Time, *with symbols of the golden wing, the third eye, the winged hourglass, and the spiraling serpent—Chronos (meant as a clockface)*

Pages 262–63
The Termite Nest *of the Acropolis with the Parthenon, the Colosseum, and the Temple of Vesta*

Pages 264–65
The Third Eye, *a tufa relief on the base of the stage of the Theater of the World*

Pages 266–67
The Gate of Jonah. *In the background, steps lead to the Gate of Love*
All: Montegiove, La Scarzuola

Giddy Skulls and Bones

Page 268
Maurizio Bottoni (born 1950)
Memento Mori, *2002*
Tempera on panel, 12½ × 9½ in (32 × 24 cm)
Inscription: They've given her up for dead so often now/ and she just laughs it off/ The way these bones with soul, tendons, muscles, and/ flesh can return to life. Every bit as often, so it is with painting/ To the health of the undertakers./ Amen
Fontanellato, Masone Labyrinth, Franco Maria Ricci Collection

Page 269
Anonymous Flemish Master
Vanitas, *second half of 18th century*
Lime wood, height 14⅛ in (36 cm)
Fontanellato, Masone Labyrinth, Franco Maria Ricci Collection

Pages 270–71
Anonymous
The Triumph of Death, *mid-15th century*
Fresco
Palermo, Museo di Palazzo Abatellis

A leering skeleton mounted on a ghostly horse caracoles above a jumbled heap of knights and noblewomen, prelates and peasants, nuns and beggars, running them through with his deadly darts without fear or favor. He is Death in all his gruesome glory, frescoed on the wall of a palace in Palermo by an unknown 15th-century master as a warning to the sinners of that splendid and wanton courtly society.

Pages 272 and 273
Paolo Vincenzo Bonomini (1757–1839)
The Bourgeois Spouses *and* The Painter, *from the series* I Macabri, *1802–10*
Bergamo, Church of Santa Grata inter Vites

Pages 274–77
Giacomo Busca (1420–ca. 1487) (?)
Triumph of Death *and* Danse Macabre, *1485*
Fresco
Clusone, Bergamo, Oratorio dei Disciplini

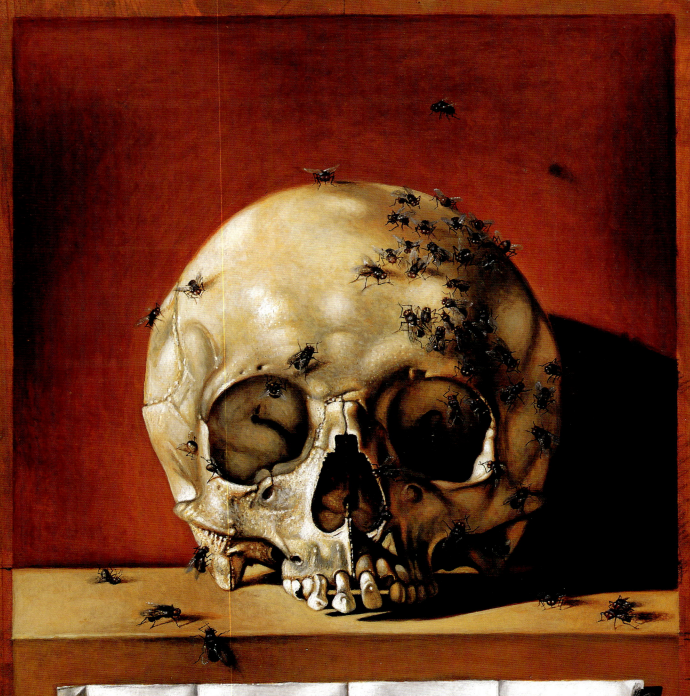

L'hanno data per morta molte volte

E lei se la ride

Come queste ossa con un anima, nervi, muscoli e

carne possono rivivere, così ogni volta la

pittura.

Con buona pace dei tanti becchini.   Amen.

Gionta la morte piena de egualeza sole uoi
ne uolza e non uolstra richeza, e pigla sono
di portar crona p che signorez ogni alcun...

Chi p...
Gl... alta b...
La morte a...
poc che m inf...

Curiosity Cabinets
and Chambers of Wonder

Shells on Parade
The Scrimshaw of Princes
The Uppsala Cabinet
Miraculous Miseroni

It is anybody's guess what gift will catch the eye of a monarch or a sovereign. These, after all, are individuals who have kingdoms or principalities or duchies at their beck and call. For instance, as Mary Dietz writes in her article "Trapping the Prince: Machiavelli and the Politics of Deception" (1986), "As the chronicler tells it, on the day Machiavelli presented *The Prince* at the palace, Lorenzo was also given a gift of greyhounds, an unfortunate circumstance indeed, for the Medici lord was more intrigued with his hounds than with princely governance." Many of the gifts presented by courtiers and diplomats to the great and the gracious were designed above all to astonish and delight. Literally, what to get the man who has everything?

The story of Europe's Wunderkammern reaches its apex with the art collection and Wunderkammer of Rudolf II of Prague. The possession of a room of wonders, a chamber of marvels, set a dynast apart. Castles and lineages are all very good; masterpieces of art are fine as well, inasmuch as they show that the powerful are also elect spirits. But a unicorn's horn? A philosopher's stone? A pet dragon? Now that's power. (Ask any Targaryen.)

The category of ivory-tower vases encompasses a very specific form of deluxe craft. Turned on a lathe—a tool that had been perfected in its modern incarnation (with continuous rotation thanks to the foot treadle) in the sixteenth century—they took the form of chalices, globes, or teetering steeples, and were topped by anything from stars and flowers to dolphins. In September 1632 a cargo of these marvels was shipped by one Medici to another (Mattias to Ferdinand, the second grand duke of his name), after they had been seized as booty by Catholic troops sacking the Lutheran city of Coburg during the Thirty Years War. And a lovely gift they must have made. Containers are a notoriously diverse category, ranging from reliquaries to pillboxes and ampules to steamer trunks. But these vases were princely outliers: objects created to contain the immaterial, just as the body contains the soul.

That same year, shortly before he was killed at Lützen in a battle that marked a watershed in that long, tedious, and exceptionally savage war, King Gustavus Adolphus of Sweden received a gift from the city of Augsburg that befitted his kingly status. It was a cabinet conjured into being by that magus of joinery, Philipp Hainhofer, adorned with alabaster, amethyst, coral, gold, pearls, rubies, and coco-de-mer.

And let us not overlook the work of the Miseroni. The best-known artisan of that workshop was Dionysio Miseroni, whom we might call the Willie Wonka of rock crystal.

In the final analysis, however, aside from considerations of the practical or the moral, thrill-seeking or personal gratification, the basis of the need for a Wunderkammer was as an example to the world: there was a hierarchy, and the Creator had meant emperors and kings to occupy the penthouse of it. As Anselmus de Boodt, gemologist to the court of Prague around the turn of the seventeenth century, wrote: "The Emperor is a lover of stones, and not simply because he hopes thus to increase his dignity and majesty, but through them to raise awareness of the glory of God, the ineffable might of Him who concentrates the beauty of the whole world into such small bodies and in them unites the seeds of all other things in creation."

Shells on Parade

Facing page
Ornamental Goblet, *German, ca. 1640*
Nacreous nautilus shell with mounting
in silver and gilded bronze, mermaids,
seahorses, chains, and a man astride
a volute (spiral shell); base with an Eastern
figure leading a lion on a leash
Florence, Museo degli Argenti

The Scrimshaw of Princes

Pages 284–85
Domenico Remps (ca. 1620–1699) (attr.)
Cabinet of Curiosities *(Scarabattolo),*
second half of 17th century
Oil on canvas, 38¾ × 53⅛ in
(98.5 × 135 cm)
Florence, Opificio delle Pietre Dure

Pages 286–87, left to right
Ornamental vase with cover
Ivory, height 19⅝ in (50 cm)
Marcus Heiden (fl. 1618–1664)
Ornamental vase with cover, *1625*
Ivory, height 23⅛ in (58.8 cm)
Marcus Heiden
Ornamental vase with cover, *1627*
Ivory, height 17 in (43 cm)
Ornamental vase with cover
Ivory, height 18¾ in (47.5 cm)
All: Florence, Museo del Bargello

Pages 288–89, left to right
Marcus Heiden
Ornamental vase with cover *(detail), 1626*
Ivory

Contrefaitkugel (Counterfeit Sphere),
Nuremberg, 1618–20
Ivory, height 8⅝ in (21.9 cm)
Inside are two miniatures, of Cosimo II and
his son Ferdinando II of Tuscany, which can
be viewed through the holes in the globe.
Ornamental vase with cover, *1626*
Ivory, height 22½ in (57 cm)
All: Florence, Museo del Bargello

The Uppsala Cabinet

Pages 279, 290, and 291
Philipp Hainhofer (1578–1647)
King Gustavus Adolphus of Sweden
Cabinet, *1632*
Crowned by a coconut shell; outer
and inner panels with floral decoration
in semiprecious stones; scenes from the
Life of Christ *painted on alabaster.*
Uppsala, Gustavianum Museum

Pages 292 and 293
Philipp Hainhofer
King Gustavus Adolphus of Sweden
Cabinet, *1632*
Uppsala, Gustavianum Museum
Note the scenes of love in all its forms
depicted on the central octagon.

Pages 294–95
Philipp Hainhofer
King Gustavus Adolphus of Sweden
Cabinet, *1632*
Concealed panels with Last Judgment
and Moses Crossing the Red Sea, *painted*
on slabs of alabaster
Uppsala, Gustavianum Museum

Miraculous Miseroni

Pages 296–97
Gasparo Miseroni (ca. 1518–1573)
Vase with Lid, *Milan, ca. 1580*
Enameled gold, pearls, and rubies;
handles with harpies in enameled gold
and precious stones, 7⅝ × 9½ × 6½ in
(19.3 × 23.9 × 16.3 cm)

Pages 298–99
Miseroni Workshop
Plate, *ca. 1600*
Rock crystal, semiprecious stones,
diameter 18 in (45.7 cm)

Pages 300–301
Miseroni Workshop
Vase with handles and lid decorated with
scenes of The Triumph of Bacchus *(detail),*
Milan, late 16th century
Rock crystal mounted on enameled gold

Page 302
Gasparo Miseroni
Goblet in the Form of a Dragon with
Handle, *Milan, ca. 1580*
Lapis lazuli, enameled gold, emeralds, rubies,
and pearls, 6⅝ × 7½ in (17 × 18.9 cm)

Page 303
Miseroni Workshop
Interior of a Bowl, *Milan, 1575–80*
Lapis lazuli, silver gilt, enameled gold,
agate, and cameo carved with Leda and
the Swan, *diameter 16½ in (41.7 cm)*

Pages 304–305
Ottavio Miseroni (ca. 1569–1624) and
Jan Vermeyen (before 1559–1606)
Tazza with Lid *(detail of lid)*
Green amethyst
All: Vienna, Kunsthistorisches Museum

An Eye for Illusion

To be tricked by a good optical illusion is like being tickled. One of the delights of *trompe l'œil* is that it evokes the deepest upswelling of emotion available, memories of childhood foolishness, while also indulging in the core entertainment of the artistic mind, synesthesia. Why is something pouring in through my eyes, theorized by the poets of chivalry as windows to the soul, suddenly making my ribs and shoulders twitch with uncontrolled laughter, or some rough equivalent thereof? Just as translators love palindromes (take it from me, a purveyor of moody doom), artists tend to love crossover short circuits between genres, limbic systems, and media.

One of the early optical realizations in the pages of Ricci's publishing house and, in short order, those of FMR, was *Musca depicta* (1982), André Chastel's magisterial book-length essay on the presence of painted flies in art throughout the Renaissance and after. Puns—the lexical equivalent to the synesthetic laugh reflex intrinsic to Op Art—abound in this connection. "A Fly in the Pigment" is the headline in issue no. 19 (April/May 1986). *There's a Fly in the Painting* was the title of the 2024 exhibition at the Masone Labyrinth and Museum; it was an intentional stab at a parody of UB40's "Rat in Mi Kitchen," which came out that year. Pascal mused on the power of flies to distract the mind "of this sovereign judge of the world," calling them "sovereign gods." Chastel focuses on the trick Giotto, still an apprentice, played upon his teacher Cimabue around 1280: painting a fly on the nose of a figure in an artwork with such verisimilitude that the great forefather of the Renaissance tried to brush it away not once but repeatedly.

All art, of course, is a trick, one that requires the willing participation of the con's target. There is perhaps no loss on the part of the gullible, but there is certainly gain on the part of the wily manipulator of vision and belief. It is no accident that literature's greatest pickpocket was known as the Artful Dodger. Andrea Mantegna bedecked his *trompe l'œil* paintings at the Ducal Palace of Mantua with flies, and the transcendent Giovanna Garzoni of Florence put them in her *Still Life with Lapdog* (1650).

A century later, *quadratura* painters specialized in creating illusory architectural space and tricky perspective. Clever visual magicians, they projected nonexistent columns and arches, lofty parapets and banisters into the viewer's own ambient space. On flat plaster, they created three-dimensional worlds. They did not come cheap, and, in fact, with their optical trickery they were to high-ticket aristocratic painting what special-effects wizards are to present-day film. The House of Este hired Antonio Viani and Jean Boulanger to crowd the walls of its castle at Sassuolo, north of Bologna, with classical gods and wondrous depictions of all sorts. That was their vacation resort and hunting lodge. Piety had ruled the roost in art throughout a more God-fearing age; now, in an age of exploration and new frontiers, the chief fear was of being thought dull, so wit was at a premium. Artists had striven to make their work believable in an age of belief, but now great lords hired the witty to deceive them. In 2022–23, the Metropolitan Museum of Art put on a show titled *Cubism and the Trompe l'Oeil Tradition*. Like a fly on a painting, inviting you to try to brush it away, René Magritte's painting of a pipe bears the ironically non-tobacco-related warning *Ceci n'est pas une pipe* (This Is Not a Pipe). Let the illusions continue!

Bridal Suite

Facing page and pages 312–13
Andrea Mantegna (1431–1506)
Camera Picta *or* Bridal Chamber, *1474–75*
Fresco
Mantua, Palazzo Ducale

Ceiling: Trompe-l'œil *oculus, from which various figures look out and down, including winged cupids, ladies, a servant, and a peacock*

Entrance wall: Left, Ludovico Gonzaga Journeys to Milan
Center: Dedication Plaque by Andrea Mantegna to His Patrons *Right:* Meeting between Ludovico II Gonzaga and Cardinal Francesco Gonzaga. *They are surrounded by other members of the family, including Emperor Frederick II and Christian of Denmark*

Fly on the Wall

Page 314
Petrus Christus (ca. 1420–1472/73)
Portrait of a Carthusian Monk, *1446*
Oil on panel, 11½ × 8 in (29.2 × 20.3 cm)
New York, Metropolitan Museum of Art

Page 315
Master of Frankfurt
Self-Portrait of the Painter with His Wife, *1496*
Oil on panel, 14¾ × 10¼ in (37.5 × 26 cm)
Antwerp, KMSKA—Royal Museum of Fine Arts Antwerp

Pages 316–17
Giovanna Garzoni (1600–1670)
Lapdog, *1650*
Oil on canvas, 18⅞ × 26¾ in (48 × 68 cm)
Florence, Palatine Gallery

This painting belonged to the Grand Duchess Vittoria della Rovere and is probably a portrait of one of her dogs.

Inlaid Illusion

Pages 318–19
Wood Inlays in the Studiolo of Federico da Montefeltro
Urbino, Palazzo Ducale, Piano Nobile

Among the rooms of the Palazzo Ducale in Urbino, the studiolo of Duke Federico da Montefeltro (1422–1482) stands out for its exquisite magnificence—a small, intimate retreat yet rich in imagery, the monastic cell of a humanist prince and military leader. Here, Federico would withdraw in the company of great minds—of philosophers, poets, and generals depicted in the paintings adorning the walls— surrounded by sacred symbols, virtues, mottos, and emblems, as well as enigmas and cryptograms. The studiolo of Urbino is a temple dedicated to the Renaissance religion of the Individual and individual Virtue. This small chamber, the most complete surviving example of its kind from the early Renaissance, is decorated in its lower register with splendid wood inlays depicting illusionistic motifs. This particular detail features musical instruments and a sword, objects that allude to the duke's varied pursuits.

Just Add Foreshortening

Page 320
Antonio Viani (ca. 1555–ca. 1635) and Jean Boulanger (1606–1660)
Room of the Este Virtues, *ca. 1640*
Sassuolo, Palazzo Ducale, Apartment of the Duke

Viani painted the false architecture simulating a loggia, and Boulanger the balcony decorated with caryatids that opens onto scenes of exploits of the House of Este. On the ceiling is the Virtue of the House of Este.

Pages 321 and 322–23
Jean Boulanger
Putti, *1650–52*
Sassuolo, Palazzo Ducale, Gallery of Bacchus, lower register

Acting as a frame to the scenes of the Life of Bacchus, *cheerful putti play with the fringed borders of the faux tapestries and hide behind them.*

· PETRVS · XPI · ME · FECIT · A · 1446 ·

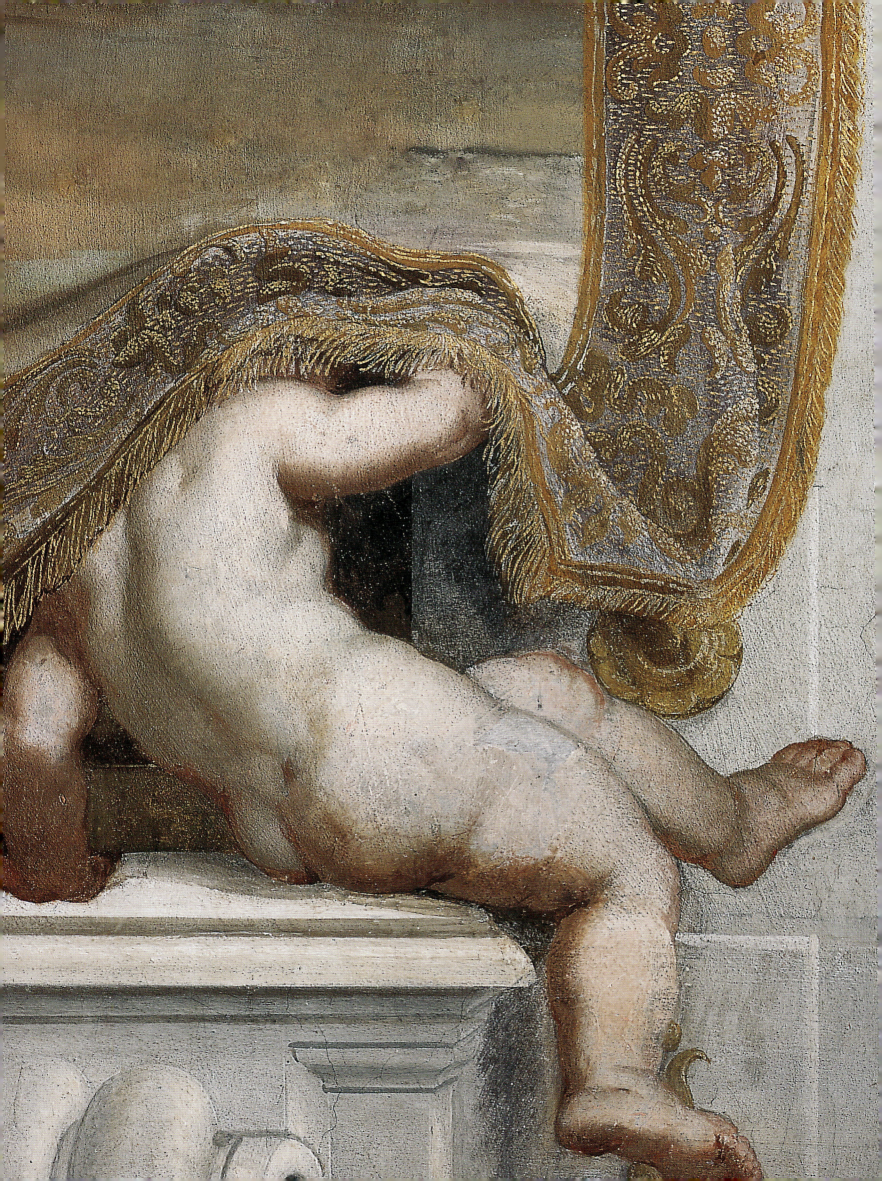

A Strange Fashion
of Forsaking

The notion of fashion carries within it a paradox. One of the oldest quests of humankind is the pursuit of the new. All that is solid vanishes into air, leaving space on the store shelves for new models, styles, cuts, and modes. If you explore a spreadsheet of the word "fashion" in every language on Earth, you will find an almost universal wall of the word *mode*: from Finnish *muoti* to Czech *móda* to Greek μόδα and Russian мода. Yet English stubbornly sticks to the strange and muscular word *fashion*, a verb you might expect to find in the poetry of Milton or Blake, but not on Carnaby Street or in Saks Fifth Avenue.

In 1923 a young man from Italy with a remarkable gift for fashioning shoes out of unexpected materials decided to set up shop in Hollywood, the same year that the HOLLYWOOD(LAND) sign first went up. He was Salvatore Ferragamo. In his autobiography, Ferragamo wrote, "Hollywood was calling. The future was calling." Specifically, the studios were calling, with creative briefs to craft footwear for ancient Egypt—curly-toed shiny sandals for Rameses II in *The Ten Commandments* (1923), for instance—and the American Civil War. Gloria Swanson, Mary Pickford, and Pola Negri were customers first as studio staff, and later as fabulous celebrities and semi-private citizens. One demanding client was an Indian princess who wanted shoes made from an unspecified material never before used to fashion shoes. Ferragamo responded to the throw-down with an éclat worthy of fellow southern Californian Dr. Seuss: by producing slippers made of hummingbird feathers.

This audacious narrowing of the boundaries between craftsman, bespoke purveyor, and visionary surrealist establishes a link between a Ferragamo and a Franco Maria Ricci. Certainly, FMR has always been open to fashion's visual appeal and culture. It featured the work of Roberto Capucci and even held an exhibition of his creations in the museum amid the Masone Labyrinth, with evening gowns resembling hummingbirds or the spectrum of vision certain species of butterfly possess (with between five and fifteen photoreceptors they can see millions or even billions more colors than the human eye). One wonders if studies should be done on the optical apparatus of the Italian designer, in his mid-nineties at the time of writing.

Philologists (the archeologists of vocabulary) note that blue was the last color to be given a name; the ancient Greeks called the sky *leukos*, the same color as a leucocyte, or white blood cell. Early settlers of Virginia called the stunning spring blooms—so obviously pink to our Pantone sensibilities—"redbuds." But imports began to arrive from India in the seventeenth century, around the same time as English dictionaries began publication. It would be interesting to track a parallel history in visual input and lexicographical output.

Experiential advances in that era included the advent of coffee, even though one suspects some substance of more hallucinogenic power to explain the visual vibrancy of the work of William Larkin and Lavinia Fontana. Feverish flourishes and furbelows abound in these paintings, especially those of Edward Sackville and of Bianca degli Utili Maselli and her children. These vignettes look like photo-renderings of some of the more advanced fashion photography of the 1990s. A word to the perceptive: all the art that appears in FMR was filtered through the lens of gifted and rigorous photographers, first and most notable among them the prolific and astute Massimo Listri.

Frills and Furbelows

Facing page
William Larkin (1580–1619)
A Baby, Said to Be Lady Waugh, *ca. 1615*
Oil on canvas, 35½ × 28 in (90 × 71 cm)
Private Collection

This is the only known portrait by Larkin of a baby. In an age of extreme infant mortality, the child must have been of exceptional prominence to merit such a commission. So far, the baby remains unidentified. The Scottish name Waugh probably belonged to the family into which the child eventually married. Here, too, we see Larkin's distinctive looped silk curtains; the carpet is the same as in his portrait of Lady Isabella Rich (ca. 1615). Dating the painting with any precision is a challenge, although the curtains place it after 1613.

Page 330
William Larkin
Philip Herbert, Earl of Montgomery, later 4th Earl of Pembroke, *ca. 1615*
Oil on canvas, 84 × 49½ in (213.5 × 125.5 cm)

This is arguably the most splendid of all Larkin's full-length portraits of male sitters, and in superb condition. It captures exactly what Edward Hyde, 1st Earl of Clarendon, alludes to in respect of Herbert, the "comeliness of his person," and the composition achieves its dazzling effect through the juxtaposition of rich fabric textures: a suit of cloth of silver, robes of crimson velvet lined with white satin, and the looped pink magenta curtains fringed with gold that frame the figure.

Page 331
William Larkin
Lucy Harington, Countess of Bedford, *ca. 1616(?)*
Oil on canvas, 30¾ × 19¼ in (78 × 49 cm)
Sweden, Gripsholm Castle

Lucy Harington, Countess of Bedford (1582–1627), was the daughter of John, 1st Baron Harington of Exton, and Anne Kelway. In 1594, she married Edward Russell, 3rd Earl of Bedford, first cousin of Anne Clifford. In her portrait Lucy is attired in peeress's robes of crimson velvet and ermine, with a countess's coronet on her head. These were certainly worn at the coronation of James I in 1603. They would have been worn again in 1610, when James I's eldest son was created Prince of Wales, but the dress here is a

decade later. The occasion, therefore, is likely to have been the creation of Henry's younger brother Charles prince in succession to his deceased brother, in Westminster Hall, London, in November 1616.

Pages 332–33
William Larkin
Edward Sackville, later 4th Earl of Dorset (detail), *1613(?)*
Oil on canvas
London, Ranger's House (English Heritage)
The Wernher Collection, Suffolk Collection

Edward Sackville (1590–1652) was the younger brother of Richard Sackville and succeeded him as earl in 1624. He was twenty-three when this portrait was painted as a pendant to that of his brother, and it is likely to record clothes worn at the wedding of the king's daughter to the Elector Palatine in February 1613. The main theme of the embroidery is roses and pansies, but perhaps the most extraordinary elements are the gauze garters and the vast golden shoe rosettes.

Symphony in Auburn

Pages 334–35
Lavinia Fontana (1552–1614)
Portrait of Bianca degli Utili Maselli and Her Children, *ca. 1605*
Oil on canvas, 39 × 52½ in (99 × 133.5 cm)
San Francisco, Fine Arts Museums
Sotheby's

The India Trunk

Pages 336–37
Garara *(split skirt), Lucknow, mid-20th century*
Silk and gold brocade, with gold gota *(lace) appliqué, length 40½ in (103 cm), waist 48 in (122 cm)*

Page 338
Jooti *(shoe), Jaipur, mid-19th century*
Leather with pearl embroidery, length 9¼ in (23.4 cm)

Page 339
Topi *(hat), Gwalior, early 20th century*
Cotton with gold zaki *(brocade), circumference 20 in (50.8 cm)*

VERGINIA

Better to Rule in Heels

Facing page
Salvatore Ferragamo (1898–1960)
Gold brocade ankle boot, stiletto heel
covered with kid, 1955–56

Pages 342 and 343 (top to bottom,
left to right)
Salvatore Ferragamo
Sandal with kid upper, wooden wedge heel
with carved and geometrical decoration,
1935–36
Sandal with crocheted raffia upper,
low cork heel, 1935–36
Sandal with satin and calf upper, platform
sole and wedge heel covered with glass
mosaic, 1935–36
Invisible, *1947*
Sandal with nylon thread upper, F-shaped
wood wedge heel covered with printed kid
Pull-over, *1966*
Shoe with silk grosgrain upper
Décolleté, *1930–35*
Upper in needlepoint lace, called
Tavernelle, similar to Venetian needlepoint;
edge of heel covered in kid
All: Fondazione Ferragamo

Chrysalis and Metamorphosis

Page 325
Roberto Capucci (born 1930)
Conchiglie, *1992*
Silk taffeta
Villa Manin, Fondazione Roberto Capucci

Page 344
Roberto Capucci
Geometrie, *1992*
Shot fuchsia taffeta, poppy red interior strip
Villa Manin, Fondazione Roberto Capucci

Page 345
Roberto Capucci
Farfalle 2, *1992*
Evening dress of cyclamen, blue, and dark
green silk taffeta with intarsia edges in
different colors
Villa Manin, Fondazione Roberto Capucci

Pages 346–47
Roberto Capucci
Farfalle, *1985*
Evening dress of green silk sauvage
taffeta plissé with turquoise, cyclamen,
red, and blue edges, and a large butterfly
on the back
Villa Manin, Fondazione Roberto Capucci

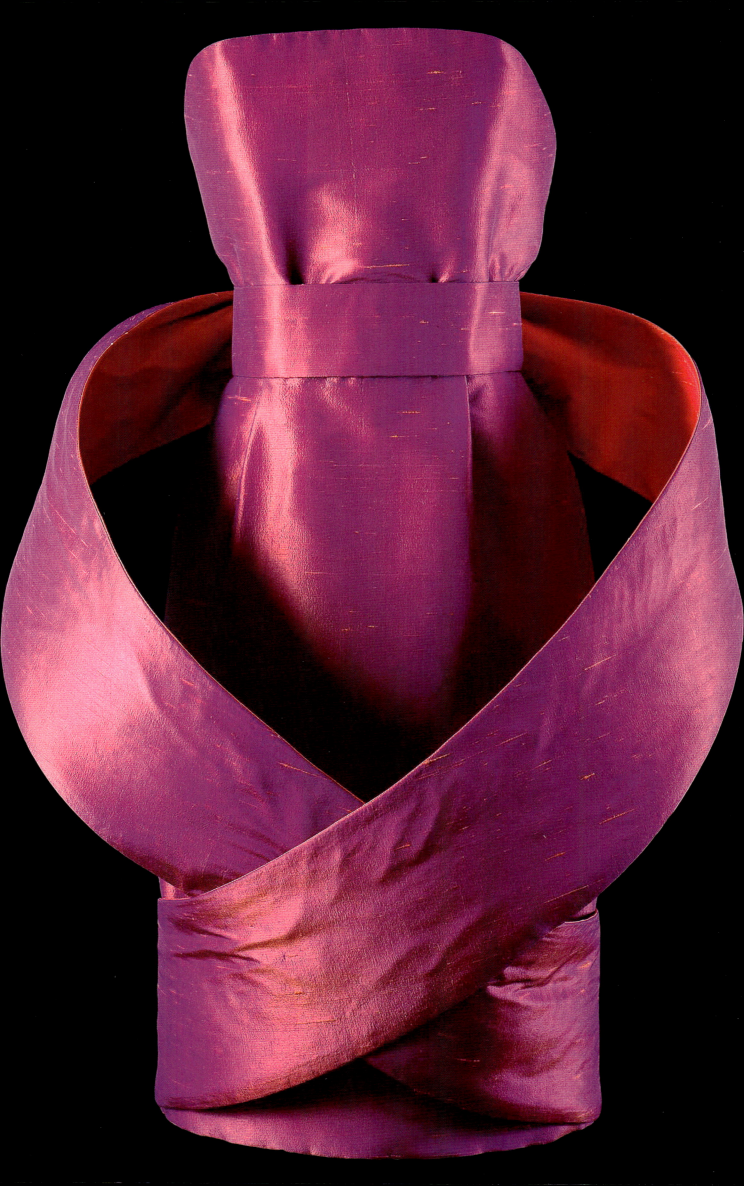

Flora and Fauna: The Humanist Eye

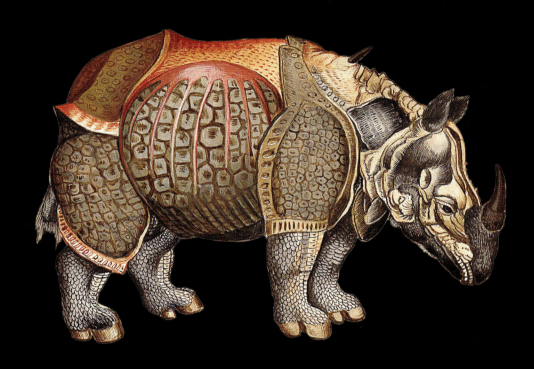

Pier Antonio Michiel
Jacopo Ligozzi
Daniel Fröschl
Nicolas Robert
Ulisse Aldrovandi
Birds of Paradise

In the era of discovery and exploration, a word was coined in English that has sadly declined since: *nondescript*. To today's ear, it's something close to dull and beige. But in the early centuries of the modern era, it meant any of the countless species of flora and fauna that had never before been seen. Not yet described, in short.

Ricci—who trained as a scientist, even if that was not his ultimate calling (although his early publishing work, in the field of magnificent and painstaking facsimiles, did draw on the science of philology)—was particularly captivated by the work of early natural historians, as scientists were then known. He focused primarily on four scientific or quasi-scientific creatives, beginning with the earliest, Ulisse Aldrovandi (1522–1605). The science writer Michon Scott offers a fantastic summary of his life on her website Strange Science. Pope Gregory XIII rose to the papal throne in 1572, whereupon a fearsome dragon promptly appeared in the Bologna countryside—a worrisome omen. Fortunately for the pontiff, he had a cousin—Aldrovandi—who happened to be a lifelong dragon aficionado and opined that a dragon augured exceptionally well. Aldrovandi, a true Renaissance man, was wedged roughly between the lifespans of Leonardo da Vinci and Galileo. *Nomen est omen*, Italians still say (to quote Latin sayings in Italy is like quoting an old-time Quaker in the United States), and Papa and Mamma Aldrovandi named their boy after the protagonist of the *Odyssey*. Dante, whose *Divine Comedy* is basically an Advent calendar of the great minds of all time, portrays brave Ulysses urging his men on to new discoveries: "O brothers! call to mind from whence we sprang: ye were not form'd to live the life of brutes but virtue to pursue and knowledge high." Ulisse Aldrovandi seems to have taken the lesson to heart. He built a highly acclaimed cabinet of curiosities containing more than 18,000 specimens, 7,000 dried plants preserved in fifteen volumes (the oldest in the world), 17 volumes of watercolors, and 14 cupboards filled with woodcut blocks. Surely, those blocks include the images that you see here.

Other names that have graced the pages of FMR in this category (and which appear here) include the great Jacopo Ligozzi (1547–1627), Pier Antonio Michiel (1510–1576), Daniel Fröschl (1563–1613), and Nicolas Robert (1614–1685). Not shown here but definitely to be savored in the pages of FMR are the flora and fauna (primarily of the avian persuasion) of John James Audubon (1785–1851), the *Book of Animals* by the fourteenth-century Syrian miniaturist Aboy Othman Amru al Kinani al Dschahif, gorgeous sixteenth-century volvelles or wheel charts for astronomical calculations and predictions, the hallucinatory botanical rebuses of Giuseppe Arcimboldo (ca. 1527–1593), and the incredible illuminated birds of Carlo Antonio Raineri (1765–1826). Last of all, the amazingly exotic flora and fauna of Aloys Zötl (1803–1887), an Austrian painter and master dyer whose *Bestiarium*, filled with watercolors of magnificent beasts, was rediscovered by the Surrealist André Breton decades after Zötl's death. Breton recognized a surrealist esthetic in Zötl's work, and called it "the most sumptuous bestiary ever seen." Last and most daunting comes Gaetano Giulio Zumbo (1656–1701), a Sicilian wax sculptor obsessed with anatomy and corruption, who created morbid and horrifically beautiful tableaux of death from plague and syphilis.

Pier Antonio Michiel

Facing page
Ciruleas monteses ex fruta de Indiani,
plate 1
Pier Antonio Michiel (1510–1576), I cinque
libri di piante. Libro azzurro (Libro de
albori. frutici et in vogli), *Cod. It. II. 26–30
(=4860–4964)*
Venice, Biblioteca Marciana

Jacopo Ligozzi

Page 354
Jacopo Ligozzi (1547–1627)
Avicennia germinans *(black mangrove)*,
plate 25
*Florence, Uffizi, Gabinetto dei Disegni
e delle Stampe (Department of Prints
and Drawings)*

*From the very start, an enthusiastic
association developed between the Medici
family and the plant kingdom, revealed
through a constant interest in varieties of
tree and medicinal plant, botanical studies,
and floral varieties. The splendid gardens
that surround the Medici palaces offer
glowing evidence of this ecological* coup de
foudre, *and the most respected witness to
this passion was Jacopo Ligozzi, a painter
and illustrator so gifted that he earned the
title "the new Apelles of nature," a reference
to the renowned ancient Greek painter of
that name.*

Page 355
Jacopo Ligozzi
Agave americana *(century plant), plate 30*
*Florence, Uffizi, Gabinetto dei Disegni
e delle Stampe (Department of Prints
and Drawings)*

Daniel Fröschl

Pages 356 and 357
Daniel Fröschl (1563–1613)
Helianthus annuus *(common sunflower)*,
plates 45 and 46
Codex Casabona, ms. HP 513bis
Pisa, Biblioteca Universitaria, Hortus
Pisanus

Nicolas Robert

Page 358
Nicolas Robert (1614–1685)
Onopordum illyricum L. *(Illyrian thistle, or
Illyrian cottonthistle, Mediterranean basub)*
Vélins, t. XXXII, n. 26
*Paris, Muséum National d'Histoire
Naturelle*

*As proud of his gardens as the Almighty
would presumably be of Eden, Louis XIV
wished their fleeting botanical riches
to be immortalized on the finest* vélin
*(parchment) and preserved in albums to
display to his most distinguished visitors.
The artist who fulfilled that desire—and
inaugurated a centuries-long collection
that is arguably the supreme masterpiece
of scientific illustration—was the painter
Nicolas Robert, an indefatigable harvester
of images, both meticulous and magnificent.
In his botanical plates, the splendor of
plants and flowers becomes a natural
mirror of the opulence of the* Grand Siècle.

Page 359
Nicolas Robert
Centaurea babylonica L. (*Syrian
knapweed*), *Asia Minor*
Vélins, t. XXXIII, n. 22
*Paris, Muséum National d'Histoire
Naturelle*

Acanthium Illyricum *capitibus majoribus.*

N. Rob. pin.

Onopordum illyricum. (Lin:)

Europe austr:

Iacea maxima Prosp.
Alp. de exot.

N. Rob. p.

Centaurea babilonica. (*Lin:*)

Orient.

Ulisse Aldrovandi

Page 349
Ulisse Aldrovandi (1522–1605)
Rhinoceros, *from* Plates of Animals, *Fondo Aldrovandi, plate 91, ca. 1570*
Bologna, Biblioteca Universitaria (BUB)

Facing page
Jacopo Ligozzi (1547–1627)
Cerastes *(horned viper) and* Ammodytes *(sand viper), 1577/1580, MS. Aldrovandi,* Plates of Animals, *vol. IV, plate 132, ca. 1570*
Bologna, Biblioteca Universitaria (BUB)

Pages 362–63
Ulisse Aldrovandi
Pica bresilica or Toucan americis *(American toucan), plate 19 from* Plates of Animals, *Fondo Aldrovandi, ca. 1570*
Bologna, Biblioteca Universitaria (BUB)

Pages 364–65
Ulisse Aldrovandi
Uromastyx *(spiny-tailed lizard), plate 129 from* Plates of Animals, *Fondo Aldrovandi, ca. 1570*
Bologna, Biblioteca Universitaria (BUB)

Birds of Paradise

Pages 366 and 367
Paradisea apoda *and* Paradisea raggiana *from* Monograph of the Paradiseidae or Birds of Paradise *by Daniel Giraud Elliot, London and New York 1873, in-folio*

Cerastes serpens perniciosissimus ex
Lybia ad serenissimum Hetruriæ
Ducem allatus una cum Ammo-
dite: Qui mihi utrumq; uiuum
donauit, et deinde etiam ambos ʒ
depictos ad me misit.

Ammodites.
Hæmorrhous, quod ictu suo uel morsu
copiosissimum e uulnere sanguinem
eliciat, ʊt Dioscorides testatur his
uerbis: ex plaga copiosus cruor efflu-
it, et quacunque parte corporis cicatrix
ʊlla fuerit ea sanguine manat.

Pica Bresilica piperiuora
Bεσιγχοs á magnitudine rostri
Longirostra.
Ramphastes
Hipporhyncos
Toucan Americis
Gaza di Bresilia Italis
Alcantras Indorum.

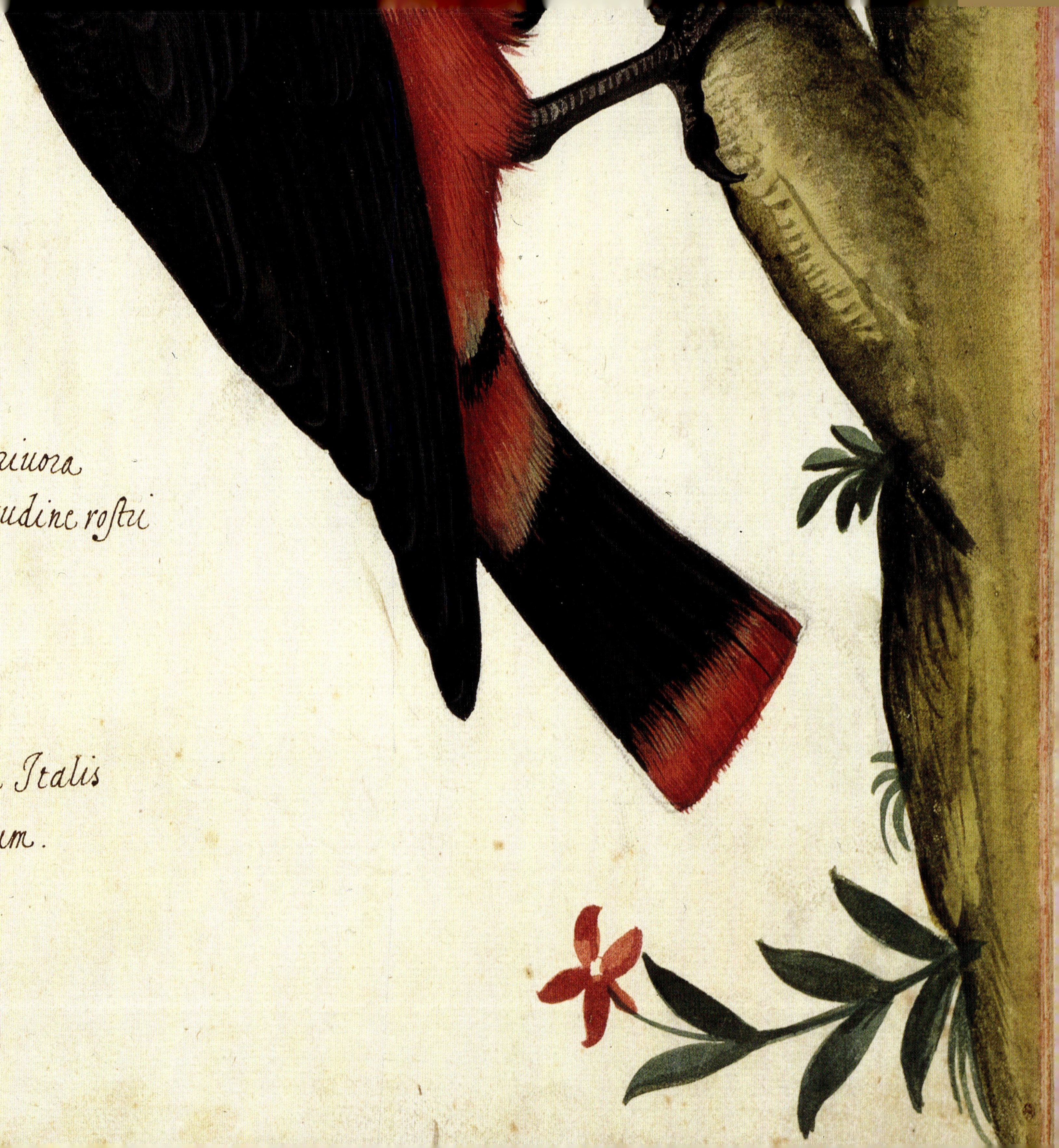

Cordylos Aristotelis, seu Cordulus.
Caudiverbera.
Vromastrx, uel
Vriomastix.
Phathages Indicus Aeliani.

2.

Art of the People

Somehow, in the glistening precincts of FMR's elegant pages, the folk arts claimed a special birthright status, recognized intuitively and hailed in choral acclamation. Whether in the form of patiently tatted lace, ingeniously crafted Neapolitan Christmas manger scenes, or the muscular carvings of sailing-ship figureheads, folk art weaves throughout the pages. Then there is a pair of commercial undertakings that seem uniquely folk-adjacent: the steamships painted by the Bard Brothers and the merry-go-round horses of Coney Island, Rocky Point, and other amusement parks. In a yin-yang inverse relationship, both pay obeisance to an older tradition of portraiture enshrined in the great country houses: the equine portrait over the mantelpiece. The Bard Brothers painted steamships plying the Hudson River, providing portraits for entrepreneurs spreading the trade that made New York City the nation's commercial capital. And the merry-go-round horses allowed children and their parents to pretend that they too possessed stables and meadows and views of the Hudson.

In this context, I'd like to tip my hat to two numinous figures in the creation of the magazine over decades. The Edgar Allan Poe and T. H. White of FMR are Giovanni Mariotti and Gianni Guadalupi, the former still in fine fettle and writing for the magazine, the latter no longer with us, but sorely missed. Mariotti is a novelist as well as an editorial wizard; Guadalupi was a connoisseur of exploration and the fantastic.

Both adored the quaint and the paradoxical. Mariotti wrote the book *Butroto* (1984) about a country that appeared on no map, a cross between the imaginary Shangri-La and the real Bhutan. He opened it with a wry observation on the nature of journalistic competition (in the days before the internet). However much each magazine thought it had an unrivaled scoop, the two leading newsweeklies of an unnamed advanced Western nation would invariably run the same story on their covers. No one knew how it happened, although speculation abounded. So when one of newsweekly A's intrepid correspondents discovered the uncharted land of Butroto, he immediately set out to beat the competition. Once he arrived, however, standing before the mist-wreathed castle at the center of the mountain fastness, what did he see but the intrepid correspondent of newsweekly B?

Guadalupi dabbled in the annals of exploration and the delights of the nonsensical. A favorite topic was uchronia (the temporal equivalent of utopia), the "what ifs" of alternate histories. Two of his books, sadly not yet translated into English, are *1938: La Distruzione di Parigi* (The Destruction of Paris) and *1308–1590: America vichinga* (Viking America; both 1984). In the first, the answer to the question "Is Paris burning?" was the deathless, "Oui, mon général!," while in the second, a Viking expedition, exploring the Mississippi basin from its imaginary base on the island of Mannahatta, marches west only to encounter a Mongol army marching east across present-day Nebraska, led by none other than Marco Polo. Guadalupi also wrote, with Alberto Manguel, *The Dictionary of Imaginary Places* (1980), a serious reference work about frivolous non-places, from Atlantis to Zenda.

Of course, these two literary adventurers worked side by side with Franco and Laura in a newsroom shared by Jorge Luis Borges and Italo Calvino, author of *Invisible Cities* (1972). In a way they might appreciate, I'd like to remember their contributions as the folk artists of FMR's editorial staff.

Paper Lace with Baby Jesus

Facing page
Baby Jesus, *late 19th century*
Needle-cut paper engraving with geometric motifs, 3½ × 5¾ in (8.9 × 14.6 cm)
Michele Falzone del Barbarò Collection

Homemade Altarpieces

Pages 374 and 375
Little Altars, *second half of 19th century*
14¾–17¾ × 11¾–13¾ in
(40–45 × 30–35 cm)
The medallions were produced with chromolithography

The Neapolitan Crèche

Pages 369 and 376–77
Scenes of Rustic Life, *details of Neapolitan crèches, second half of 18th century*
Private Collection

Page 378
Giuseppe De Luca (1876–1950)
Elderly Peasant Woman, *detail of Neapolitan crèche, turn of the 19th century*
Private Collection

Page 379
Nicola Somma (dates unknown) (attr.)
Tavernkeeper, *detail of Neapolitan crèche, late 18th or early 19th century*
Private Collection

Marble Diorama

Pages 380–81
Giovan Battista Firrera and Nicastro Di Giovanni
Antependium of the Chapel of the Madonna Libera Inferni, *before 1685*
Marble, agate, Venetian glass mosaic tiles, and semiprecious stones
Palermo, Church of the Immaculate Conception

Pages 382–83
Domenico Magrì and Filippo Dedia
Antependium of the Chapel of San Benedetto, with little temple, *ca. 1691*
Marble, agate, Venetian glass mosaic tiles, and semiprecious stones
Palermo, Church of the Immaculate Conception

The Gun-Toting Angels of Cuzco

Page 384
Master of Calamarca
Dominion, *17th century*
Oil on canvas, 64⅜ × 45 in (163.5 × 114.2 cm)
Calamarca (La Paz), Parish Church

The scepter and crown this angel is holding enable us to identify him as a Dominion, the second order of celestial choirs. Dominions govern the heavenly bodies and earthly elements.

Page 385
Master of Calamarca
Uriel Dei, *17th century*
Oil on canvas, 63½ × 43 in (161.5 × 109.5 cm)
Calamarca (La Paz), Parish Church

Uriel Dei, seen here loading his arquebus, from which a long fuse dangles, is dressed in red and green: traditional iconography would have shown him holding a fiery sword. He is the fourth of the seven main archangels found throughout the West, and is also worshipped in the Orthodox churches. He is identified with the virtue of prudence and the gift of knowledge.

Page 386
Master of Calamarca
Letiel Dei, *17th century*
Oil on canvas, 64⅜ × 44¼ in
(163.5 × 112.5 cm)
Calamarca (La Paz), Parish Church

Page 387
Master of Calamarca
Gabriel Dei, *17th century*
Oil on canvas, 63½ × 43⅛ in
(161.5 × 109.5 cm)
Calamarca (La Paz), Parish Church

Gabriel means "the strength of God"; he was the guardian of the heavenly treasure, the teacher of the patriarch Joseph, and the angel of the Annunciation. Traditionally, although not in this case, he is represented with a bunch of lilies. Here, Gabriel Dei is wearing a uniform similar to that of Charles II's royal guard: a long cassock-like garment known as a chamberga (redingote), with very wide sleeves, and an enormous flamboyant plumed hat. On his right shoulder he carries the pole of a checkered banner, the end of which he is holding with his other hand.

American Figureheads

Facing Page
Benmore
Newport News, Virginia, The Mariners' Museum

When it was launched in 1871, the British ship Benmore *was adorned with a mythological figurehead. In 1920, after the ship became American-owned, the figurehead was repainted by its patriotic owners to represent Columbia (or America). It still wears the same colors today.*

Page 390
Saucy Sally
This is not a figurehead but in fact a stern-carving that decorated the outboard rudder of a late 18th-century Dutch vessel. Mystic, Connecticut, Mystic Seaport Museum

Page 391
Double figurehead
Despite the abundance of ships with double names in the 19th century, only a few double-figure figureheads survive today. It remains unknown whether this carving comes from an American or a foreign ship. Mystic, Connecticut, Mystic Seaport Museum

Pages 392 and 393, left to right
Magdalena
The largest figurehead in the collection of the Mystic Seaport Museum. It comes from the schooner Magdalena, *built in 1889 by R. Napier & Sons in Glasgow for the Royal Mail Steam Packet Co. The* Magdalena *was one of the last British liners to be built with a concave bow, making it also one of the last ships to carry a figurehead. Mystic, Connecticut, Mystic Seaport Museum*

Great Admiral
The three-masted Great Admiral *was launched in 1867 at the Robert E. Jackson shipyard in Boston. The ship was named in honor of naval hero David Glasgow Farragut, who had been appointed full admiral by an Act of Congress in 1866. It remains unknown whether Admiral Farragut himself or a photograph of him served as the model for the figurehead. Mystic, Connecticut, Mystic Seaport Museum*

Donald McKay
A figurehead depicting a Scotsman that adorned the clipper Donald McKay, *launched in 1855 at the McKay shipyard in Boston. The ship was built for British shipowner James Bain. Mystic, Connecticut, Mystic Seaport Museum*

Seminole
A full-length figurehead depicting a Native American, belonging to the ship Seminole, *built in 1865 by Maxson & Fish in Mystic, Connecticut. The figurehead was likely carved by the Campbell & Colby company, just 1 mile (1.6 km) from the museum's present location. Mystic, Connecticut, Mystic Seaport Museum*

Steamboats on the Hudson

Pages 394–95
John and James Bard (1815–1856 and 1815–1896)
Robert L. Stevens, ca. 1836
Oil on canvas, 35½ × 22 in (90.2 × 55.9 cm)
Newport News, Virginia, The Mariners' Museum

The Carousel Animals of Charlotte Dinger

Page 396
Charles Looff (1852–1918)
Sea Dragon, *ca. 1905*
Length 7 ft (2.1 m)
Florida, Albert Ricci Collection

Page 397, from top
Stein and Goldstein lead horse, *ca. 1912*
Gold and silver leaf blends with patina of body paint
Morristown, New Jersey, Charlotte Dinger Collection

Philadelphia Toboggan Company tiger, *ca. 1905*
A rare menagerie figure with original body paint
Morristown, New Jersey, Charlotte Dinger Collection

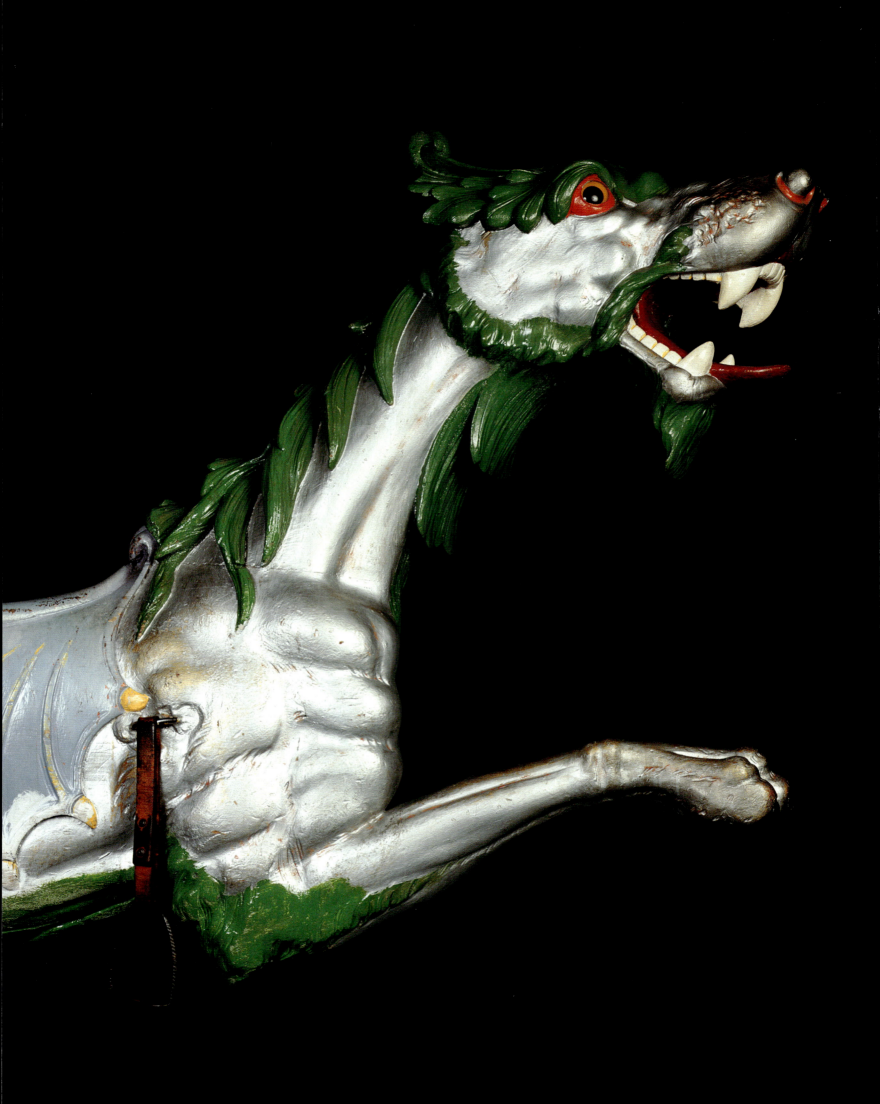

The Past Is a Foreign Country

That Totonac Smile
That Qajar Poise
A Venetian Merchant at the Mughal Court
Tagasode: Gold, Silk, and Changing Screens

The core gestures of courtesy—the bow, the curtsey (itself a corruption of "courtesy"), the hand-kiss, and the handshake—are all thinly disguised bobs and squints of submission or, at least, of truce. An openly extended hand contains no dagger, a bow-and-scrape offers the nape of the neck to the executioner's sword, a groveling kowtow actually inflicts damage in an anticipatory willingness to suffer in fealty. The court itself, a historical throughline of military dominance, reached its apex in the era of empire, the mid-eighteenth century and all of the nineteenth, when the hollow square was the dominant infantry formation: self-similar structures, especially if architects use the terms "court" and "square" interchangeably.

The epitome of gorgeous Persian art, the paintings of the Qajar era (1796–1925) coincided with a time of tension and fear. The chief proponent and patron of Qajar art, Fath-Ali Shah, took the Peacock Throne in 1797, following the assassination of an uncle. He imposed a rigid code of etiquette, a word related to the English "ticket" in the sense both of a pass offering admission and of a listing, in this case of "ceremonial observances at a court." Nothing bespeaks etiquette like a rigidly posed portrait, and Qajar art flourished like Topsy at Fath-Ali's court. The fabrics and faces are entrancing; Fath-Ali soaked up various forms of culture like a sponge. He was given a set of the third edition of the *Encyclopædia Britannica* on the occasion of his coronation, and he determinedly read through all eighteen volumes, thereafter adding to his list of glories and appellations the phrase "Most Formidable Lord and Master of the Encyclopædia Britannica." (It is worthy of note that the *Britannica* was both a manifestation of empire and the creation of Scots based in Edinburgh: the most ferocious members of the British empire, so fierce that the Romans refrained from invasion and instead built a wall to keep them out.)

Consequently, this expression of Persian national and dynastic refinement and beauty, as is so often the case, was distilled and compressed in a crucible of strife, fear, and invasion (viz. the Russo-Persian wars of 1804–13 and 1826–28). To quote Harry Lime, the character played by Orson Welles in *The Third Man* (1949), in a line written by Welles himself, "In Italy for thirty years under the Borgias, they had warfare, terror, murder, and bloodshed, but they produced Michelangelo, Leonardo da Vinci, and the Renaissance. In Switzerland, they had brotherly love, they had five hundred years of democracy and peace, and what did that produce? The cuckoo clock." The sentiment is admirable, although the facts are somewhat muddy; cuckoo clocks were traditionally made in Bavaria.

Artistic excellence is often prompted by the effort to ignore or transcend times of war. The dazzling Tagasode changing screens shown on pages 416–17 date from the Edo period (1603–1868), which ushered in a time of peace but followed more than a century of strife among rival warlords in Japan.

In 1653, a Venetian teenager named Nicolò Manucci ran away from home. Fifty years later, after a life almost impossibly full of adventure, he sat down to write a history of the Mughal empire, based on his first-hand knowledge of the court of Aurangzeb, last of the Great Mughals. To illustrate his history he commissioned a series of miniatures by Indian artists, some of which appear here.

That Totonac Smile

Pages 403–407
Totonac sculptures, South Central Veracruz,
Mexico, Late Classic Period, AD 600–900
Sand brown clay, originally painted with
plant pigments, height ca. 15¾ in (40 cm)
Xalapa, Museo de Antropología

The cheerful appearance of these sculptures
likely has religious-sacrificial significance.

That Qajar Poise

Page 408
Lady of the Court Playing a Drum,
beginning of 19th century
Oil on canvas, 69⅞ × 41 in (177 × 104 cm)
London, Victoria and Albert Museum

Page 409
Mother and Son with Parrot
Style of Muhammad Hasan Khan,
beginning of 19th century
Oil painting, 43¾ × 31½ in (111 × 80 cm)
Formerly in the Amery Collection
Tehran, Negarestan Museum

The mother is dressed in the European
fashion, with a parrot perching on her
right hand and a naked baby in her
lap; a beautiful vase of flowers stands
prominently by the windowsill in the
background.

Pages 410–11
Lovers Drinking
Style of Mohammad Sadiq, end of
18th century
Oil painting, 24 × 30¾ in (61 × 78 cm)
Formerly in the Amery Collection
Tehran, Negarestan Museum

The young man holds a carafe, apparently
of Persian origin, as is the young woman's
glass. She gazes somewhat knowingly at
the viewer.

A Venetian Merchant at the Mughal Court

Page 412
First depiction of Vishnu, *15r*
"*This so-called deity has various names*
and has performed many actions that are
as infamous in the eyes of men as they
are unworthy of divinity—as can be read
in the account of the Hindu religion in
the third book of my History. 1) Figure of
Vishnu; 2) Cows, always depicted alongside
this false deity; 3) Ox, likewise always
accompanying the god; 4) The god's three
wives, who are always with him and are
half-woman, half-serpent; 5) Serpent, upon

which the god rests, holding its tail in his
hand; 6) Pond with flowering banks, the
usual dwelling place of the god; 7) This
false deity has various names, as I have
already mentioned, and is called Krishna,
Parashurama, Narasimha, and yet other
names." (Nicolò Manucci, Codex Ita VI 136
B.N. Marciana, Venice, *14v*)

Page 413
[Portrayal of the grief experienced by
a Hindu woman upon learning of her
husband's death] *69r* "*1) The widow weeps*
for her loss and displays the signs of her
deep sorrow; 2) Her mother embraces her
to express her shared grief; 3) Four women,
relatives of the widow, mourn alongside her,
demonstrating their sorrow through cries
and wailing, with their hair disheveled; 4)
The widow is stripped of all the jewelry she
wore while her husband was alive; 5) Two
women remove her jewelry; 6) The widow
bathes; 7) Another woman assists her, and
after the bath, her head will be shaved. 8)
The bangles that the widow has removed."
(Nicolò Manucci, Codex Ita VI 136 B.N.
Marciana, Venice, *68v*)

Pages 414–15
[Battle Scene] *8v (detail)*
The miniature has no caption; it belongs
to the banjara *series and depicts a battle.*

Tagasode: Gold, Silk, and Changing Screens

Pages 416–17
Tawaraya Sōtatsu (fl. ca. 1600–1643)
Waves at Matsushima, *17th century*
Six-panel folding screens: ink, color,
gold, and silver on paper, 60 × 143¾ in
(152.2 × 365.2 cm)
Washington, DC, Freer Gallery of Art,
Gift of Charles Lang Freer, F1906.231–232

Pages 399, 418–19
Whose Sleeves?, *late 16th–early 17th*
century (right-hand screen); early to
mid-17th century (left-hand screen)
Pair of six-panel folding screens: ink,
color, and gold on gilt paper, each screen
57 × 136½ in (144.9 × 346.8 cm)
New York, Metropolitan Museum,
H. O. Havemeyer Collection, Bequest of
Mrs. H. O. Havemeyer, 1929, 29.100.493.494

15

Caserta:
A Palace to Contain
the World

The English Garden
A Grand Perspective
Diana and Actaeon
The Staircase of Honor

The Palace of Caserta is one of the most monumental royal residences in Europe, one of the last great estates modeled on the styles perfected both in central Italy (Latium and Tuscany) and in Spain (with its Alhambra and Generalife). That makes perfect sense inasmuch as it constitutes the mainland capital of the peculiarly named Kingdom of the Two Sicilies, a metaphysical impossibility that grew out of an age-old rivalry between a not-yet-unified Italy and an ascendant and sprawling Spain, a Habsburg empire that first laid claim to Sicily and southern Italy under the houses of Aragon and Anjou with the War of the Sicilian Vespers (1282–1302). The short version is that the Kingdom of Sicily had managed to keep its mainland domains but had lost the fabled island. It might not still control Sicily, but it continued to call itself the Kingdom of Sicily and, when it finally regained the island itself, monarchic accounting could count that only as the acquisition of yet another Sicily, this one real; but the long-cherished theoretical Sicily prevailed by right of seniority.

That odd duality makes the Palace of Caserta—the great creation of Luigi Vanvitelli and the cadet branch of the House of Bourbon that ordered it built —a domain in the mind as well as at the base of the shin of the Italian boot. But imagine if you'd grown up just outside of the walls surrounding it. That is the premise of *Il desiderio di essere come tutti* (The Desire to Be Like Everyone; 2013), a book by Francesco Piccolo that won Italy's most prestigious literary prize, the Strega. Piccolo is also well known as co-screenwriter, with the novelist Elena Ferrante, of the television series *My Brilliant Friend* (2018–24).

"I was born one day in the early summer of 1973, at the age of nine," he writes. Evening was falling, and he and two friends had climbed over a wall and were now wandering freely, juvenile outlaws, around the grounds of Caserta. There was a refrigerator packed with "chocolate-nut ice cream cones, Cokes, orangeades, mineral waters—anything you could possibly want." But, more importantly, "there was the Palace, completely empty, but we hadn't come here for the Palace. If the other two kept quiet—when they did finally keep quiet, in a pause amidst all their excitement—you could clearly hear the slow, faint sound of the water in the waterfall, which was a very gentle waterfall. A sound that I had never before perceived so distinctly." He was perched at the highest and most beautiful spot in the palace grounds, with the waterfall behind him and the graceful swoop of the landscaped slope stretching out to the majestic building with its 5 stories and 1,200 rooms. "Practically speaking, for an instant there entered into my head an intuition that matched that solitude and yet, at the same time, negated it; at the very moment that I was alone in the world, I started to notice that I *wasn't* alone in the world. It seemed to me, for one hallucinatory instant, that all the walks and all the grounds were completely overrun by hundreds of thousands of people, millions of them, walking from the suites of the Palace uphill toward the waterfall, and that these were all the human beings that had ever set foot in the Palace from the day it had been built until this very afternoon. And I was there too, in their midst."

This is the idea at the core of FMR. Every page of the book you now hold, every one of the roughly 40,000 pages of FMR in all its editions—English, Italian, Spanish, and French—has been frequented and inhabited by the Thousands, by the Millions, and you gaze at it in vast and rapt company.

The English Garden

Page 421
Grotto with a Nymph
Royal Palace of Caserta, English Garden

Facing page
Bath of Venus
Royal Palace of Caserta, English Garden

A Grand Perspective

Pages 426–27
View of the Royal Palace of Caserta
from the Fountain of Venus and Adonis
by Gaetano Salomone

Diana and Actaeon

Pages 428–29 and 430–31
Paolo Persico, Angelo Brunelli, Tommaso
and Pietro Solari, and Andrea Violani
(all fl. 18th century)
Fountain of Diana and Actaeon
Royal Palace of Caserta

The group with Diana surrounded by her
nymphs is on one side of the waterfall's
basin, while the group with Actaeon
transformed into a stag is on the other.

The Staircase of Honor

Pages 432–33
Grand Staircase with lower and upper
vestibules
Royal Palace of Caserta

Lions in white Carrara marble,
modeled by Tommaso Solari and
carved by Paolo Persico, on either
side of the Grand Staircase.

I Am Just a Boxer

The Resting Fighter
Rome's Stadium of Marble Athletes

In our early, quasi-clandestine days of conceptualizing this book, my colleague Pietro Mercogliano and I talked about structuring the entire volume as a labyrinth. That proved perhaps excessively and needlessly intricate. Maybe we should have been thinking not of Daedalus and the Minotaur (who were we, after all, to try to vie with James Joyce, who named his literary alter ego Stephen Dedalus?), but rather of Ulysses (a "man of twists and turns," according to Robert Fagles's version or, in Emily Wilson's somewhat world-weary rendering, "complicated"). Ulysses. Bring it, James Joyce. We'll take the title, not the narrator. And so, in a sense, let me, with my unindicted co-conspirator Pietro, describe here and now the twofold composition of this book: a maze (*lab´yrinthos*) but also a voyage of return, a homecoming (*nóstos*). After all, every issue of FMR is planned and conceived in a surprisingly short and intense burst of creativity. There is preparation, of course, but the actual bout with each issue is like an act of improvisation. I like to say that while FMR is filled with art from the ages, be they ancient or surprisingly recent, it is in fact—in the context of each issue writ large over the decades—an omnibus of exploits, a late twentieth- and early twenty-first-century *oeuvre* of performance art. It was true when Franco and Laura were assembling it, and it remains true in the New Series of FMR that began in 2021.

Or perhaps it's an act of athletic bravura, like a boxing match. There are lines in the great Paul Simon song "The Boxer" that evoke the Hemingwayesque stance assumed by the creators of this magazine, single-handedly setting forth a way of seeing, an alternative history of Western art. (The philosopher and politician Benedetto Croce once said that the history of art was ultimately created by the bindery workers who stitched together folios of illustrated pages, printed in four colors of ink—or five for FMR— into bound, ordered volumes.)

"In the clearing stands a boxer," the song goes, and there is a line that, paraphrased with "see" for "hear," might well have described Ricci's method: "Still a man hears what he wants to hear." Franco and Laura are towering figures in the way that they stubbornly persisted, almost indifferent to the crosscurrents of cultural change. The early issues of the magazine look just as timely and of the moment as do the latest ones. Timely, and timeless.

We mentioned the word *nóstos*, going home. In the end, Franco was determined to build a labyrinth of his own on the family land he knew best. Outside of Fontanellato, he built the largest bamboo maze on Earth, his own personal pyramid, a watchtower overlooking the labyrinth, and a world-class museum, as we have noted. Home was a farm in the richest agricultural region of Italy, a place of civilized retreat but unexampled sophistication, the personification of what the Romans called *otium*.

To quote Robert Louis Stevenson, as much a kindred spirit uniting Ricci and Borges as might have been Cervantes or Diderot or Bodoni, "Home is the sailor, home from sea./ And the hunter home from the hill."

The athletic figures shown here begin with a bronze boxer from the Baths of Constantine in Rome, a public facility that offered the comforts of civilization until the sixth-century Gothic War, when virtually all water to the Eternal City was cut off by cunning Ostrogoths. They continue with marble athletes from the Foro Italico, in keeping with the overstated "art pompier" style of Italy's official art in the 1920s and 30s.

The Resting Fighter

Facing page and pages 440–41 (detail)
Statue of a Boxer from the Baths of
Constantine on the Quirinal Hill, Rome
Bronze, height 50⅜ in (128 cm)

The boxer is depicted at rest in the minutes
following a bout: the powerful figure
sits, relaxed, his body leaning forward
in an interplay of complex and unstable
equilibriums. The face, portrayed with
heightened realism, carries reminders
of the athlete's brutal pursuit: right eye
swollen from the blows of fists, the ears
cut and mangled, and the nose flattened
and torn. The body, shaped with acute
sensitivity to anatomical detail, features
the powerful musculature of a torso in
contrast with long, lithe legs—all traits
typical of long training in the art of
boxing. The distinct coloration of hair and
beard, the rendering of an evocative and
expressive disquiet in the facial features,
and, most of all, the virtuoso, baroque
details of the massive musculature point
to an artistic composition dating from the
late Hellenistic period (4th–1st century BC).
Similarities in the figure's spatial placement
and beautifully shaped physique can be
found in an ancient marble sculpture: the
Belvedere Torso in the Vatican, signed by
"Apollonios, son of Nestor, Athenian," who
worked in Rome in the first half of the
1st century BC. Indeed, this bronze boxer
is commonly attributed to Apollonios,
an eclectic artist of late Hellenism.

Rome's Stadium of Marble Athletes

Page 435
Aldo Buttini (1898–1957)
Boxer at Rest
Donated by the Province of Chieti
Rome, Foro Italico, Stadio dei Marmi
(Stadium of Statues)

Page 442
Giuseppe Cecconi (fl. 20th century)
Boxer *(detail)*
Carrara marble, height ca. 13 ft (4 m)
Donated by the Province of Ascoli Piceno
Rome, Foro Italico, Stadio dei Marmi
(Stadium of Statues)

Page 443
Aroldo Bellini (1901–1984)
Discus Thrower *(detail)*
Carrara marble, height ca. 13 ft (4 m)
Donated by the Province of Imperia
Rome, Foro Italico, Stadio dei Marmi
(Stadium of Statues)

Pages 444–45
Nino Cloza (1890–1960)
Shot-Putter *(detail)*
Carrara marble, height ca. 13 ft (4 m)
Donated by the Province of Piacenza
Rome, Foro Italico, Stadio dei Marmi
(Stadium of Statues)

Materials
and Composition

Wood • Ivory • Fabric • Glass
Wax • Terracotta
Gold • Bronze • Porcelain
Marble • Leather

If you calculate an average of four long articles and three short two-page items for every issue of FMR, and round it out to about 200 issues among the various languages (to say nothing of companion magazines, such as *KOS* and *Poiein*), you have at least 1,400 subjects of physical art. It's an *omnium gatherum* worthy of Ricci's paragons, the publishers of the great Enlightenment *Encyclopédie*.

But there's a throughline of materials, and the understanding that the centuries from which those articles draw had a varying assortment of materials in which to work. Marble (not to be confused with travertine), pietra serena (found in Florentine architecture but also a leitmotif in the background of Florentine portraits), or even the products of exploration (coco-de-mer, the material of sea coconuts, or giant nautilus shells embellished with precious stones and gold and silver bases to make spectacular tabletop conversation pieces, all brought back from the great Southern Sea).

Ezio Manzini, in his pioneering book *The Material of Invention* (1986), talks about the traditions of matter and the ways in which it becomes material. Granite, oak, bronze: Manzini calls these mute materials. He speculates about the differences between the natural and the artificial, a pyramid and a sand dune, a hut and a bird's nest. The book ranges from the rectangular slab that marks the opening scene of *2001: A Space Odyssey* to the bioengineering of the androids in *Blade Runner*. He also notes that, for the first time in human history, we're creating materials that don't exist in nature, and designing them to meet their uses. It is some of the most sophisticated new materials that sink their roots deepest into the past: plastics can be used to make toy models of dinosaurs, a genuine ouroboros in that the plastic was made from oil distilled from the composted bodies of dinosaurs. Similarly, in the Grand Tour of the eighteenth and nineteenth centuries, aristocratic British tourists would come to see the great volcano overshadowing Naples, then have their likenesses—or other more traditional motifs—produced in volcanic sulfur intaglios.

Here we've arranged artworks in a continuum of materials: wood, fabric, glass, ivory, terracotta, wax, porcelain, marble, and gold, to name just a brief sampling.

Later in his career, Manzini reflected soberly on the difference between old, traditional materials and new, custom-manufactured ones. It was a surprising take: no one *loves* plastics, he said; the only materials people *love* are the materials that need us. Plastic is prideful and indifferent to human beings in its injection-molded perfection. But brass beds, leather boots, and wooden tables all *need* human beings, to polish them to a brassy gleam, to apply mink oil to make them pliant and comfortable to walk in, to rub in wood oil to give them a lustrous glow. Traditional materials (unlike many human beings, as Mark Twain pointed out) are capable of gratitude and desirous of our help. If they are also artistically beautiful, well, then that love is in some sense requited.

Facing page
Wood
*Wood Inlays in the Studiolo of Federico
da Montefeltro*
Urbino, Palazzo Ducale, Piano Nobile
*This small study, the most complete
example of the genre to survive from the
early Renaissance, is decorated, in its lower
register, largely with depictions of library
cabinets standing ajar; inside them, it is
possible to see books and other objects.*

Page 452
Ivory
Salerno Tablets
Salerno, Museo Diocesano
*Upper panel: "And it came to pass in
those days, that there went out a decree
from Caesar Augustus, that all the world
should be taxed.... And Joseph also went
up from Galilee...to be taxed with Mary
his espoused wife, being great with child"
(Luke 2:1, 4–5).*
*Lower panel: "When they had gone, an
angel of the Lord appeared to Joseph in a
dream. 'Get up,' he said, 'take the child and
his mother and escape to Egypt. Stay there
until I tell you, for Herod is going to search
for the child to kill him!'" (Matthew 2:13).*

Page 453
Fabric
Bernard van Orley (1492?–1542)
Invasion of the French Camp *(detail)*
Cartoon
Naples, Museo Nazionale di Capodimonte
*A mysterious, beautiful woman walks off
the battlefield. She seems to have emerged
unscathed and well groomed.*

Page 454
Glass
The Portland Vase Base Disk, *first half of
the 1st century* AD
*Translucent blue and opaque white cameo
glass, cut down from a larger composition,
diameter 4¾ in (12.2 cm)*
London, British Museum
*A young man is seen in profile, the
forefinger of his right hand raised to
his chin in doubt or consternation.*

Page 455
Wax
Seal of Charles Emmanuel III of Savoy,
King of Sardinia
*Red wax, diameter 5 in (12.9 cm), thickness
¾–1 in (2–2.5 cm), weight 13¾ oz (346 g)*
Vatican Archives

Pages 456 and 457
Terracotta
Niccolò dell'Arca (ca. 1435–1494)
Compianto sul Cristo morto (Lamentation
over the Dead Christ)
Polychrome terracotta, life-size
*Details of Mary of Clopas (Cleophas)
and Mary Magdalene*
Bologna, Church of Santa Maria della Vita

Page 458
Gold
Seal of Henry VI (1165–1197), recto/verso
*Bright yellow gold, Type 2; diameter 2¼ in
(57 mm), thickness ⅛–¼ in (1.5–4 mm),
weight ½ oz (12 g)*
Vatican Archives
*The second son of Frederick Barbarossa,
Henry was, over time, King of the Romans,
Holy Roman Emperor, and King of Sicily*

Page 459
Bronze
Gian Lorenzo Bernini (1598–1680)
Solomonic (barley-sugar) column, *1633*
Rome, St. Peter's Basilica, Canopy

Page 460
Porcelain
Gio Ponti (1891–1979)
Hand figurine, Exorcism, *1935*
Hand figurine, Flower blossoms, *1935*
Porcelain; height 13⅜ in (34 cm)
*Sesto Fiorentino, Museo delle Porcellane
di Doccia*

Page 461
Marble
Tomb of Francesco Bartolomeo Tomasi
Valletta, Church of St. John the Baptist
*Epitaph: "This is the tomb of Knight
Commander Francesco Bartolomeo Tomasi,
son of Nicola, a nobleman of Cortona, a
member of the holy ranks of the Knights of
Malta, and devoted to their service by land
and sea from the year 1708 until his death;
he always acted with great faith, and lived
seventy-nine years and six months and
eighteen days. Laid in the peace of the Lord
on 21 April 1768. Mindful of death, he had
his tomb built while he was still alive."*

Pages 462–63
Leather
*Personal binding created for Maximilian
of Saxony for the Bodonian edition of*
Orazione recitata nell'Istituto delle scienze
di Bologna..., *dated 1794*
Madrid, Biblioteca Nacional

455

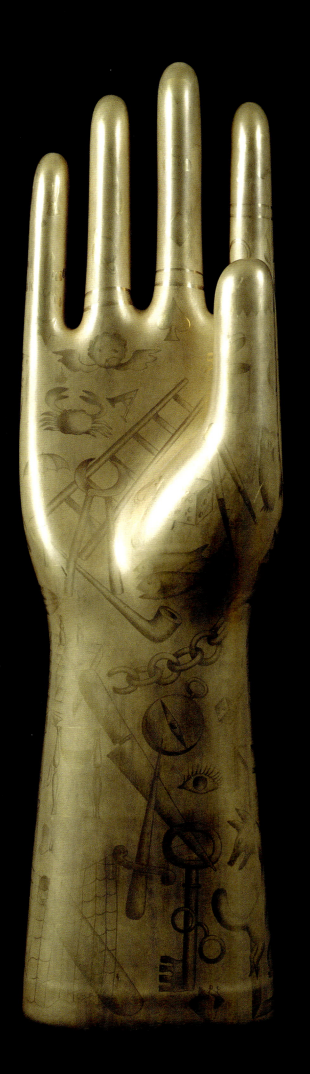

MORS.ULTRA
NON.DOMINABITUR

A.   ☧   Ω.
BAJUL.FR.BARTHOLOMAEUS.NICOLAI.FILIUS.THOMASIUS
DOMO.CORTONA.URBIS.SUAE.PATRICIUS
HEIC.SITUS.EST
SACRAM.EQUITUM.HIEROSOLYMITANOR.MILITIAM.PROFESSUS
EJUSQUE.AB.ANNO.CIↃIↃCCVIII.SERVITIO.ADDICTUS
TERRA.MARIQUE.DONEC.VIXIT
OFFICIUM.SUUM.SUMMA.FIDE.PRAESTITIT
VIXIT.ANNIS.LXXIX.MENS.VI.DIEB.XVIII.
DEPOSITUS.IN.PACE.☧.DIE.XXI.MENS.APR.AN.MDCCLXVIII
MORTIS.MEMOR
HUNC.SIBI.VIVENS.TITULUM.POSUIT

Operation Columbus
21 June 1984

Creating works of art has long required salesmanship as well as technical prowess: just ask Brunelleschi, Michelangelo, and Cellini. Brunelleschi, in particular, found an advanced engineering solution to the challenge of the dome for Florence's cathedral, one so remarkable that it took near-hypnotic powers to persuade his fellow Florentines to work without scaffolding (suffice it to say that it involved employing the engineering principles behind the Chinese fingertrap to place stone blocks in a structure weighing over 25,000 tons, teetering atop a direct drop of thirty-eight stories). That took some strength of will.

To launch FMR in the United States, Ricci had to persuade his fellow Italians to underwrite a massive direct-mail and advertising campaign costing many millions. His plan was to use other people's money (especially that of banks) to print 8 million blads, or offprints of the magazine, most consisting of sixteen pages and a smaller number of thirty-two pages. The final operation was smaller than that, but he did print blads in great numbers. He then had them folded into various national newspapers, including the Sunday *New York Times*. The thirty-two-pagers were touted in advertisements in many high-circulation magazines, offering the advertising supplement for $1.25. Those ads ran in *New York*, *Vanity Fair*, *Connoisseur*, *House & Garden*, *Commentary*, *Harper's*, *The Atlantic*, *Geo*, *The New Republic*, *San Francisco*, *The New Criterion*, and other magazines.

In order to print such a massive number of blads, Ricci charged tourism boards, chambers of commerce, major marketers, and consumer products companies something close to $10,000 a page for advertisements on the back cover and both inside covers, for a print run of 10,000. Had the print run really been 8 million, that would have added up to a jaw-dropping budget of $24 million (especially astonishing in those days, and in those dollars). The actual operation was less lavish.

Still, it brought in plenty of subscriptions. The exact numbers were never clear, but the claim was confidently advanced that, counting all the different editions—Italian, English, Spanish, and French—FMR was now the largest art magazine on Earth, as well as the most beautiful. Who can say? One thing was certain: that Franco Maria Ricci was one of the boldest and most tireless art publishers in this or any other century. Henry Ford is notoriously quoted as saying: "When I see an Alfa Romeo go by, I tip my hat." Let other art publishers similarly honor the memory of the Marchese Ricci, a charismatic visionary who had more fun and created more joy while making money than seems entirely reasonable.

FMR ❀

Keepsake

*of the presentation
in America
of Italy's most
beautiful magazine*

*New York Public Library
June 21, 1984*

To the Reader

This Libro d'Oro* was printed for two reasons: to celebrate the publication of FMR in English, and to honor and thank the Sponsors, without whom a small publisher like me, whose only strength lies in the unusual nature of the things I do, would never have been able to show America my magazine.

FMR is the first European cultural publication to be launched in America; it is therefore worthwhile to explain how and why it was born, but first of all I should like to discuss the reasons that brought about the Italian edition in March of 1982.

In the 1970s I began to think about the lack of a true art magazine in my country. The art magazines that did exist paid more attention to events, to the markets, collectors, and personalities of the art world than they did to the beauty of the actual works of art. They had been conceived on the same models as news magazines, and they presented generic journalism along with meager, obvious, and poorly printed images. They seemed incapable of communicating the emotion behind seeing, knowing, or reading. To survive they did not hesitate to pair Guernica with advertisements for a local painter, or to set works by Michelangelo beside announcements for an antiques show.

For these magazines, it seemed that art ended with local artists, and antiques went no further than photographs of armoires. It seemed incredible to me that an era that had produced so many visual publications in the service of fashion, furnishing, and sex was unable to produce a visual magazine dedicated to art, which is, after all, meant to be seen. While great exhibits drew remarkable crowds and fine art books sold out

quickly, the circulation of "art" magazines hovered at relatively low levels.

At this point, I decided it would be possible to create the magazine I had envisioned. I had always traveled widely for my books, meeting critics and authors, perusing manuscripts in ancient libraries, exploring the storehouses of museums, without neglecting occasional appearances at elegant parties or an evening or two in the clubs. In the course of my work, I had gone on what was called in the eighteenth century the Grand Tour.

I believed that all this—my inquisitiveness, my friendships, the discoveries I had made during my travels, my years as a graphic designer, and my awareness of the problems and techniques of printing— could lead to only one outcome: the creation, as I immediately said to myself and then to others, of "the most beautiful magazine in the world." The only thing that held me back was the fear that the people who collected my books might be scandalized at my involvement in the dubious glories and the public eye of the newsstand.

I do not believe, however, that this has happened. I believe that my collectors have become the most faithful readers of the magazine, and that they found intact in it the elegance, the taste for discovery, and the intellectual honesty that had seduced them in the limited editions.

Naturally I tried to eliminate from FMR the things I disliked in other magazines: collaboration with an art market that is largely unreliable, sloppiness in the reproduction of images, carelessness and haste in the selection of authors and texts. I wanted perfect images, and to ensure that I would have them, I had

new photographs taken whenever possible of monuments, paintings, codices, to avoid recourse to photographic archives. I asked great authors to write for my magazine, beginning with Borges, Calvino, Eco, Arbasino, and the late Julio Cortázar, who had already worked with the publishing house, as well as authoritative and well-known scholars. Being first a publisher of books, I was able to apply formal standards of books to FMR: notes, bibliographies, the pairing of scholarly texts with literary ones.

In FMR, I was determined that there would be none of the mad projects I had seen in other art publications, such as attempting to explain Bernini with one column of text and two postage-stamp-sized images. I insisted on monographic articles made to be looked at, studied, preserved.

I was proud when I learned that FMR's article on the unpublished drawings of Turks by Jacopo Ligozzi had been color-xeroxed and distributed in an art course at Princeton University. This kind of thing may happen again, and perhaps already has, since FMR often presents little-known and seldom-studied topics. It was my wish that my magazine, like my books, should have the aura of discovery.

Up to now I have spoken about the Italian edition of FMR—with its circulation of 80,000—yet the reasons for this American adventure were similar. Americans have everything but I knew that America did not have a magazine like mine, and this was confirmed by intellectuals, opinion makers, marketing experts, and my cosmopolitan friends. Essentially, the defects I had found in the European magazines, or what seemed defects to me, were not all that different on the other side of the Atlantic.

I felt that even in the United States—where a love of art was proven by the proliferation of exhibits and museums, and by the great number of people who came to see them—there was no great magazine for the cultivation of art and the image, and that therefore there was room for FMR. Indeed, the project acquired a new fascination. FMR in English could become the prestigious cultural periodical that the world seemed to lack.

But how was I to introduce it? How was I to launch it? In America, which is large, you cannot be small—no one will notice you. I was small, and unknown to the American public. The opportunity was there, but by myself I had no power to seize it. Yet it seemed that the undertaking, if it were successful, would not be only to my advantage. FMR could become an ambassador of Italian taste and culture, not in a sporadic fashion, like a concert tour of La Scala, but permanently and continuously.

I had an idea: I decided to link the introduction of FMR to a great promotion of my country in the United States. To this end, I would approach those in Italy who would be most receptive to the project: the banks.

A monk in the Middle Ages wrote that after the year 1000 Europe was covered by a mantle of churches: at the end of the second millennium, one might say that Italy is covered by a mantle of lending institutions. I counted more than a thousand of them. Most operate in areas that have a remarkable wealth of art treasures and natural beauty, although they receive few visitors. I was sure that the directors of these institutions would gladly help me tell America about the cities, the villages, the territories from which they drew their profits.

I asked each of the banks to take out a page devoted to its city

in the Preview Issue, displaying a masterpiece of art. The eight million Preview Issues could have presented the largest showcase of Italian art ever seen, emphasizing the unity of the Italian banking system in an unprecedented promotional campaign.

The idea seemed so good to me (and still does) that I immediately decided to publicize it in full-page advertisements in daily newspapers. Perhaps a less frank and public approach would have been more fruitful. Indeed, some of my friends have suggested that my idea might have been better received had I been affiliated with a political party, although I refuse to believe this. Another explanation could be that I merely outlined the program to the banks. My idea was simple but it was also quite new, and new things must be explained thoroughly. Or perhaps I did not succeed because many banks had no branches in the United States, so were not interested. It is also possible that many local banks are comfortable in the conviction that they have done enough to promote tourism and the arts in their regions when they contribute to the Feast of Turtledoves or when they fund a marching band. One cannot expect all bankers to be Cosimo de' Medici!

What amazed me most was the southern Italian banks' lack of response. The South has deep links with the United States—most of the Italians who crossed the Atlantic at the turn of the century in search of work, freedom, and wealth came from its regions. I have great respect for the Italy of sentiment and dialect that lives on in the memories of many Italian-American families, but I think it is important to remind the new generation, amply represented in the universities of the United States, that their country of origin is not just a land of sunshine and poverty, but the home of an ancient and complex civilization—a fatherland of the mind and soul, as well as of the heart.

Nonetheless, my gratitude toward the few banks and public institutions that understood my aims and accepted my invitation is as deep as their number is small. (The names of their directors appear in the complete list of sponsors published in this Libro d'Oro.)

I would especially like to mention a person to whom I am deeply grateful: Felice Gianani of ABI, the Association of Italian Banks. That I did not succeed in carrying out the program as I originally conceived it still causes a certain bitterness, but this is tempered by the fact that we were successful in launching FMR in America. Where the banks were lacking, entrepreneurs came forward to purchase many pages of FMR's Preview Issue, thus becoming the principal sponsors of the operation. The pages that were meant to display Giotto, Gaudenzio Ferrari, or Serpotta to America instead showed clothing, perfumes, wines, and jewelry.

I am not sorry that this happened. I am glad that at the end I found my partners among people like myself, who do the same work that I do and with whom there was simple and direct communication. I say "like me," even though several of them operate on a much larger scale than I. What we have in common is the same stubbornness in defending the quality of our products, the same need for new ideas, horizons, and spaces, the same impatience with bureaucratic complications and red tape.

On the other hand, many of my sponsors are small entrepreneurs from the Italian provinces, and their companies are of modest dimensions; they constitute, in terms of business and industry, the equivalent of those local banks to which I first appealed. Perhaps the same impulse that first led me to attempt this American adventure led them to become my sponsors.

I would like to add that I am happy I was able to present, through

To the Reader

the Preview Issue of FMR America, a window on the modern Italy that has made so many friends in the world through the quality of its products.

Thousands of American readers noticed the small legend accompanying the advertisements for FMR that appeared in the national press: "This page has been sponsored by Montedison in support of the arts and Italian culture." I would like to thank Mario Schimberni, the president of Montedison, and Carlo Bruno, director of public relations, information, and advertising, for their generous offer to fund FMR's entire press campaign in the United States. This offer gave me courage when courage was perhaps about to fail me; it helped me to rediscover that pride, persistence, drive, and toughness—toward oneself and, when necessary, toward others—that distinguish the true businessman.

I also owe a debt of gratitude to Umberto Nordio, president of Alitalia, Luca Cordero di Montezemolo of Cinzano, and Orazio Bagnasco of Ciga Hotels for the vital presence of their companies in the Preview Issue of FMR America. FMR is aimed at that invisible elite that knows how to appreciate perfection of detail and elegance of nuance. One Italian in a thousand purchases FMR; if this statistic holds in America, I will be content.

I would like to show Americans the little-known treasures of our artistry, and I will present those that are part of everyone's memory and culture through photography unlike any now available. We shall thus create a desire to visit Italy—not only the Italy of St. Peter's in Rome, the Palazzo Vecchio in Florence, and the Canal Grande in Venice, but also that of the frescoes of Correggio in Parma, the Baroque of Lecce, the mosaics of Piazza Armerina. I will present the research of our scholars and the talent of our writers, of today and of the past, many of whom will be translated for the first time.

These are the principal aims of my adventure.

FMR is not meant only to introduce us to America; it is meant to introduce America to us as well. Although we know much—perhaps too much— about the art produced in America in recent years, we know precious little (despite several recent exhibits) of the art that flourished in the centuries preceding Rauschenberg. We intend to explore that art with a curious and careful gaze. We shall examine American "primitives" in the same way we consider Flemish and Sienese "primitives." Our views may prove a surprise to Europeans; they may prove a surprise to Americans themselves.

To be brief, the American edition of FMR is born from the Italian edition, but it will reflect on the Italian edition as well, enriching it with other topics and other images, new texts and authors. If next year FMR France and FMR España come out, the circulation of ideas and enthusiasm among the various editorial staffs will be a further source of enrichment. A basic feeling of unity between Europe and America is more common than one might suppose. As far as it can, FMR would like to encourage that feeling.

There are those who deplore the abundance of books, magazines, films, and television shows that are exported to Europe from America. I like them, and I would like America to have an equal abundance of European books, magazines, records, films, and television programs. I hope that the path FMR has blazed will be followed by other European publishers.

I would like to thank once again those who have participated in "Operation Columbus." I hope they are pleased to see the names of their companies in the complete list of sponsors and their pages from the Preview Issue of FMR America reproduced once again. And I also hope that this Libro d'Oro will be

preserved as a worthy and interesting catalogue of advertising graphics.

I would like to conclude by thanking my collaborators, both in Italy—in the heart of the publishing house — and in Cambridge, where Professor Pietro Corsi of Harvard University guides an American editorial staff.

Alienis pedibus ambulamus ("We walk with the feet of others"), as the Romans said; I cannot count the number of friends who have contributed to FMR's success and who have lent FMR—better than feet—wings to fly to America. Among them, a special thought goes to Giorgio Armani, J. Carter Brown, Fabio Fabbri, Federico Fellini, Vartan Gregorian, Stanley Marcus, Riccardo Muti, Jacqueline Kennedy Onassis, Giorgio Orlandini, Diana Vreeland, and all those who have worked on FMR in Italy and America. My special thanks go to Giulio Andreotti, Italy's Minister of Foreign Affairs, and to His Excellency Ambassador Sandro Petrignani. To all of them, my thanks in this moment of jubilation.

Franco Maria Ricci

*The Libro d'Oro, or Golden Book, was a commemorative keepsake of the evening at the New York Public Library's reading room, complete with a list of sponsoring banks and other entities.

Excipit: Diomira and Memory

Hope may be the thing with feathers, as Emily Dickinson wrote, but it only perches in the soul. Memory won't stay still for a second. It's constantly flitting around the garden of our remembered worlds. Hope and memory have driven this revisitation of FMR, a magazine and an idea that were formative in everything I've done since (including my return as English-language editor to the New Series).

A key element of that legacy has been translation. FMR contains more translated texts than most magazines. It's where I got my start, and I've made my living as a literary translator for almost fifty years now, so I have some ideas about how translation works. After all, no original author ever sat down to write a book without an unreasonable spring of hope; along I come, months or years later, a historical reenactor trying to evoke that spirit of inspiration and infuse it into the same book, but one created after the fact in a different language.

Hope, meet memory. To conjure up an old book in a new suit of linguistic clothing, I dabble in both those emotional strains, while relying on a third: coincidence. Without coincidence and luck, translation is impossible.

Coincidences are constantly springing up and bouncing around my desk while I translate, but translating demands intense concentration. By the time the day's work is over, those delightful intersections of meaning and phoneme, idiom and lexicography have long since flown the coop. One, though, has been lingering.

It starts with Gianni Rodari, a journalist, poet, children's author, and educator. He was also someone who took immense delight in coincidences and unlikely pairings, finding in them the generative grammar of the imagination. Born in 1920 in northern Italy, he grew up under Fascism, the enemy of all things lightsome and fanciful. So when World War Two ended and he could finally express himself freely, he spread the wings of his imagination and wrote some of Italy's favorite children's literature.

Despite the clichéd image of a translator weighing the exact word with all the time in the world, if you're going to make a living by it, time is always in short supply. You must be inventive, thorough, accurate—and quick. So the first time I met Diomira Jacobini, I was too busy to understand.

The encounter was in a short story by Rodari, from his magnum opus, *Telephone Tales* (1962). The story is called, self-referentially, "Telling Stories Wrong." In it, a grandfather wants to read his newspaper, but he's been press-ganged into telling his beloved granddaughter the story of Little Red Riding Hood. So he decides to have some fun. After misnaming the heroine twice, first as Little Yellow Riding Hood, then as Little Green Riding Hood, he changes the grandmother to an aunt with a silly name. In Italian, it was "Zia Diomira."

As the translator, I am always happening along in the author's footsteps with no real idea of where I am in their story. I can see the words on the page, and I have a reasonable grounding in Italian life, culture, literary history, and language. Blithely unaware of just how special a name Diomira was, I decided to go with Hildegard. "Now go to Aunt Hildegard's house and take her this potato peel," Little Green Riding Hood's mother instructs her in my translation.

Off she goes, and in the woods on the way, Little Black Riding Hood (third mis-telling!) meets a giraffe. The granddaughter finally loses patience and asks for a quarter to buy some bubble gum. The grandfather heaves a sigh of relief and goes back to his newspaper.

That name, Diomira, hovered in my mind. I felt sure I'd done the right thing. Hildegard is a name with a specific cultural weight, a precise hint of old-fashioned aunts. Only after the book had gone to press did I discover there was more to the name than I'd guessed.

Italo Calvino's *Invisible Cities* opens with a description of the conversations between Marco Polo and Kublai Khan. The great Mongol emperor doesn't believe everything the young Venetian tells him about his travels. Yet, as Calvino writes, "The Tartar emperor does continue listening to the young Venetian with greater attention and curiosity than he shows any other messenger or explorer of his." And I realized that this book, too, was about hopes and memories. Calvino explains that the emperor has learned that his empire, which once seemed "the sum of all wonders," is actually "an endless, formless ruin." But, in Polo's tales, Khan "was able to discern the tracery of a pattern so subtle" that it could outlive loss: time's loss, entropy's loss, misunderstanding's loss.

Enthralled, I turned the page to read about the first invisible city, the first tale Polo told his rapt listener, master of all China and the grandson of Genghis Khan. Under the heading "Cities and Memory," I read these words: "Leaving there and proceeding for three days toward the east, you reach Diomira, a city with sixty silver domes, streets paved with lead, a crystal theater, a golden cock that crows each morning on a tower."

This, then, was Diomira. But the city's real quality, Polo continues, is that "a man who arrives there on a September evening, when the days are growing shorter and the multicolored lamps are lighted all at once at the doors of the food stalls and from a terrace a woman's voice cries ooh!", well, that man will feel "envy toward those who now believe they have once before lived an evening identical to this and who think they were happy, that time." I was stunned. This wasn't Aunt Hildegard. This was Diomira, and I had to learn more.

Diomira Jacobini was a film actress whose career spanned the years from 1913 to 1933. Her name appears in yet another book, by Alberto Moravia. This Diomira is less elevated: a morally dubious young woman who steers the protagonist of *Time of Desecration* (1982) into the oldest profession: prostitution. But then, that was Moravia's style.

Somehow, though, Jacobini lingered in the memories of three great writers. Moravia, born in 1909, would have been in his early twenties when her career ended; Rodari and Calvino would have been, respectively, thirteen and ten, although her films would have continued to circulate. The "tracery of a pattern so subtle," then. A name, a face, a time in a young person's life. That tracery is the influence of art, a fleeting memory, an obsessive return. It's everything we seek out in the worlds of language and imagery.

I found one of Jacobini's films online: *The Last Night* (1928). She is indeed very beautiful, especially in profile, but I'll never be able to figure what, if anything, she meant to Rodari and Calvino, although I suspect I have a better idea of Moravia's literary intentions.

It's the delicate tracery of memory that most intrigues me. There's a scene in *Citizen Kane* (1941), the story of a search for a great man's hidden longings and attachment. It is a detective story about memory, and Kane's personal business manager, Mr. Bernstein (Everett Sloane), has this to say: "A fellow will remember a lot of things you wouldn't think he'd remember. You take me. One day, back in 1896, I was crossing over to Jersey on the ferry, and as we pulled out, there was another ferry pulling in, and on it there was a girl waiting to get off. A white dress she had on. She was carrying a white parasol. I only saw her for one second. She didn't see me at all, but I'll bet a month hasn't gone by since that I haven't thought of that girl."

When Calvino wrote *Invisible Cities* sometime before 1972, Fellini's *Amarcord* (I Remember: 1973) was in the works. The delicate tracery of memory and influence might connect a scene from that movie and a memory of Diomira Jacobini. This is pure speculation. I don't know enough about this Diomira to say. Her older sister, Maria, was arguably a bigger name. At one point Maria played Joan of Arc, and her offspring have been active producers ever since in Italy's film industry (although largely under different surnames).

In *The Last Night*, lovely as Diomira's character, Alaine, may have been, it was Karina Bell (playing her maid Leontine) who captivated me. That is because when she goes to the bakery, she goes through a series of dumbshow facial expressions to coax a loaf of bread out of the baker, in defiance of rationing laws. In those features, she reminded me of the heartbreaking smiles and pouts that Georgia Hale puts on in her first screen test in 1929 for *City Lights* (1931), just a year later.

Trying to reconstruct the delicate tracery of influence in works and lives from the past is a fine and obscure art. Every time I venture onto that terrain, I'm reminded of how difficult it was to grasp the explanations of ancient Greek jokes during my college studies of the classics. "It's a reference to the leading sandal maker in Thessaly!" Um, okay. But which Diomira was it?

Wikipedia, which offers a wonderfully accessible but almost certainly unreliable portal to the trivia of the past, suggests a couple of seventeenth- and eighteenth-century nuns—Maria Diomira del Verbo Incarnato and Diomira Allegri—and, intriguingly, Diomira Magni, an equestrian acrobat who owned her own wildly popular circus. There was a Diomira in Fabio Campana's tragic three-act opera *Giulio d'Este* (1841). There are 396 Diomiras living in Brazil today. (I thank the all-knowing Giovanni Mariotti for these last two nuggets.) But ultimately, there is no saying where the wisps of knowledge, the flame-built cathedrals of inspiration, sink their roots in the minds of others. Even authors and artists may have mistaken ideas of their own sources. It makes the heuristics of translation little better than a guessing game. The best thing to do is to broadcast confidence and try not to make any howlers.

Still, the thought of Diomira prompts an image from Fellini's *La Dolce Vita* (1960): Valeria Ciangottini's portrayal of Paola, an angelic young waitress from Perugia, who first busies herself in a seaside trattoria (to the music of Nino Rota, so strongly reminiscent of Chaplin's *City Lights*), where Marcello Mastroianni is trying to focus on writing an article, and later waves a forlorn farewell to him across a narrow inlet, unable to make herself heard across the roar of the waves. Very much like the end of the same director's *La Strada* (1954), where Anthony Quinn's Zampanò stares up into the darkness, his cries drowned out by the waves. All art is just our best effort to be heard over the roar of time's ocean.

Acknowledgments

I'm immensely grateful to my fellow publishers at Vendome Press for their suggestion that we create this anthology of our FMR. It has forced me—allowed me—to unpack pearls I hadn't revisited in years. As we all know, pearls should be brought out and worn, or their light will fade and be dulled. Likewise, that is true of beauty, even the most secret varieties of beauty: made not to lie hidden, but to be brought into the light, and to gleam with splendor.

In times like these, it might seem anachronistic to produce a book that runs over so abundantly with lush loveliness. But it is precisely in an era as accustomed as we are to ugliness and injustice that it seems appropriate to seek out beauty and share it with others, that beauty should serve as a factor of disquiet, a nettlesome grain of sand itching away at our apathetic consciences, a gambit prompting a sense of wonder, as unassuming and luminous as a pearl.

LAURA CASALIS RICCI

The author and curator of this book would like to thank all institutions, private collectors, friends, and collaborators who helped dig into the past, allowing the creation of this anthology of themes and images from the various issues of both the Italian and English editions of FMR magazine.

Their thanks go to:

Aachen: Treasury of the Cathedral
Baltimore: Walters Art Gallery
Beijing: The Palace Museum
Brussels: Musées Royaux d'Art et d'Histoire
Calamarca, La Paz: Parish Church
Detroit: The Detroit Institute of Arts
Florence: Galleria Palatina; Museo Nazionale del Bargello; Museo Salvatore Ferragamo
Florida: Alberto Ricci Collection
Guanajuato, Mexico: Museo de la Alhóndiga de Granaditas; INAH (Instituto Nacional de Arte e Historia)
Hanover: Kestner Museum
Heidelberg: Kurpfälzisches Museum
Indre: Church of Saint-Marcel
Lisbon: António Horta Osorio
London: The British Museum; Victoria and Albert Museum; Mario Lanfranchi
Mainz: Mittelrheinisches Landesmuseum
Mariefred: Gripsholm Castle
Mexico City: Instituto Nacional de Bellas Artes
Milan: Galleria d'Arte Moderna

Mulhouse: Collection Schlumpf, Musée National de L'Automobile
Mystic, CT: Mystic Seaport Museum
Naples: Museo di Capodimonte
New York: The Metropolitan Museum of Art
Newport News, VA: The Mariners' Museum
Otterlo: Kröller-Müller Museum
Padua: Biblioteca Civica
Paris: Musée du Louvre; Bibliothèque national de France; Muséum National d'Histoire Naturelle
Perpignan: Jean-Claude Baudot
Philadelphia: Mr. and Mrs. Bruce Toll
Rome: Foro Italico; Luigi Serafini
Siena: Pinacoteca Nazionale
Surrey: The Goodwood Collection Trustees
Taipei: The National Palace Museum
Tehran: Negarestan Museum
Tortona: Cassa di Risparmio di Tortona
Venice: Biblioteca Nazionale Marciana
Vienna: Kunsthistorisches Museum; Osterreichische Galerie Belvedere
Zurich: Schweizerisches Landesmuseum

Photo Credits

Franco Maria Ricci: A Labyrinth of Beauty
First published in 2025 by The Vendome Press
In collaboration with Franco Maria Ricci Editore, Fontanellato, Italy

Vendome is a registered trademark of The Vendome Press LLC

VENDOME PRESS US
PO Box 566
Palm Beach, FL 33480

VENDOME PRESS UK
Worlds End Studio
132–134 Lots Road
London SW10 0RJ

www.vendomepress.com

ISBN: 978-0-86565-468-6

PUBLISHERS Beatrice Vincenzini, Mark Magowan, and Francesco Venturi
EDITOR Rosanna Fairhead
PRODUCTION MANAGER Amanda Mackie
DESIGNER AND PICTURE RESEARCHER Laura Casalis Ricci

Library of Congress Cataloging-in-Publication Data available upon request

Distributed in North America by
Abrams Books
www.abramsbooks.com

Distributed in the rest of the world by
Thames & Hudson Ltd.
6–24 Britannia Street
London WC1X 9JD
United Kingdom
www.thamesandhudson.com

EU Authorized Representative
Interart S.A.R.L.
19 Rue Charles Auray
93500 Pantin, Paris
France
productsafety@vendomepress.com
www.interart.fr

Printed and bound in China

FIRST PRINTING

Front cover image
Benozzo Gozzoli (ca. 1421–1497)
Procession of the Magi, 1459–64
Detail of King Caspar's train (portrait
of the young Lorenzo de' Medici)
Fresco
Florence, Palazzo Medici Riccardi

Pages 467–69
Franco Maria Ricci and Laura Casalis
Ricci at the launch event of FMR
America, New York Public Library
main reading room, June 21, 1984.